The Road Called Life

Lessons for the Journey

Elder Vaughn Morton

Copyright 2017 by Vaughn Morton
The book author retains sole copyright to
his contributions to this book.

Author may be contacted through Truth Ministries, Inc.
580 Pierce Ave., Clovis, CA 93612
booksbytruthministries@gmail.com

Published 2017.
Printed in the United States of America.

All rights reserved.

No portion of this book may be reproduced, stored in a retrieval system, or transmitted in any form or by any means – electronic, mechanical, photocopy, recording, scanning, or other – except for brief quotations in critical reviews or articles, without the prior written permission of the author.

ISBN 978-1-943650-62-0

Scripture quotations are from the
King James Version of the Holy Bible.

Cover Design: Aaron Marquez, AMARQUEZ.DESIGN

Additional copies available in online bookstores.

Published by BookCrafters, Parker, Colorado.
www.bookcrafters.net

DEDICATION

I dedicate this book to my boys,
Mark and Nathan,
who have been on this journey with me
for over 50 years. They have stuck by me
in life through thick and thin. Boys, may this
book help you to finish out your journey.
I love you!
~ Dad

SPECIAL THANKS

I could not have undertaken the project of this book by myself. I want to say **a great big thank you**, first of all, to Teresa (Smiley) Wodoslawsky and her husband Tim. Sis. Wodoslawsky was a great help in giving her time and patience. Her heart was really in this project, and I appreciate it. Also, thank you to Sis. Opal Shepherd, Sis. Sandi Dillon, Sis. Story Wodoslawsky and Bro. Galen Gregg. I want these people to know that I deeply appreciate their help in editing this book. I appreciate the advice and guidance of Bro. Kenneth Bow. Thank you to Aaron Marquez from AMARQUEZ.DESIGN for designing the cover and Bro. Richard Cantu for providing the image of me in my rocking chair. Oh yes…. Bro. O.C. Marler was a big inspiration and encouragement in this endeavor.

TABLE OF CONTENTS

Introduction..1
Please Remember...3
Lesson 1   Reality..9
Lesson 2   Climber, Camper or Quitter....................11
Lesson 3   Against the Wind....................................14
Lesson 4   Are We Doing the Best We Can?...............15
Lesson 5   Doing What We Don't Want to Do............17
Lesson 6   Dealing with a Problem..........................22
Lesson 7   We Can't Un-ring A Bell.........................24
Lesson 8   Tragedy of a Broken Home.....................26
            One Story from the Divide
            by Nathan Morton...................................31
            Beauty for Ashes
            by Teresa Wodoslawsky...........................37
Lesson 9   We Can't Allow the Past to Decide Our Future..41
Lesson 10   The Game Is Only Half Over...................43
Lesson 11   God Doesn't Expect Us to Fix Everything..45
Lesson 12   God, It's in Your Hands.........................47
Lesson 13   God's Time..50
Lesson 14   Heavy Sack...51
Lesson 15   The Cowboy..53
Lesson 16   Hurry Up, Sun Up...................................54
Lesson 17   The Mulligrubs.......................................55
Lesson 18   Joy! Joy! Joy!..57
Lesson 19   If You Are Not Part of the Problem...........59

Lesson 20	Let Me Alone	61
Lesson 21	Me, Myself and I	63
Lesson 22	Tree Bent Out of Shape	66
	I've Been Down That Road Before	68
Lesson 23	Just Deal with It	70
Lesson 24	Forbearing One Another	72
Lesson 25	Just Keep On Living for God	74
Lesson 26	Learning Our Lesson the First Time	78
Lesson 27	Learn What to Pay Attention To	79
Lesson 28	True Blue	80
Lesson 29	Life	81
Lesson 30	Life Can Be a Circus	82
Lesson 31	Life Takes Time	84
Lesson 32	The Unexpected Cross	87
Lesson 33	A Helpless Feeling	90
Lesson 34	Loneliness	92
Lesson 35	Lonely Times	98
Lesson 36	Dealing with Losses	100
Lesson 37	Change	102
Lesson 38	Seasons	105
Lesson 39	Old Age	107
Lesson 40	It Will Never Be Like It Was	111
Lesson 41	Sorting It All Out	113
Lesson 42	One Day at a Time, Brother, One Day at a Time	115
Lesson 43	The Stress of Life and Balance	117
Lesson 44	Money Answereth All Things	123
Lesson 45	The Time to Be Happy Is Now	126
Lesson 46	Fulfilling Our Purpose	130
Lesson 47	There's No Perfect Situation Life Is Full of Adjustments	132
Lesson 48	Timing	136
Lesson 49	Are We in Transition?	139

Lesson 50 Winning...141
Lesson 51 Working Through the Process.................142
Lesson 52 The Present Duty Is the Will of God........147
Lesson 53 The Will of God Is Not Always
           Comfortable..149
Lesson 54 You Will Know It When You See It...........151
           Bridge Builder...154
Lesson 55 A Good Understanding Makes for
           Long Time Friends..................................155
Lesson 56 Old Friends...158

"If I had a flower for every time I thought of you,
I could walk through my garden forever.".................160

~ *Long and Winding Road* by Mickey Mangun..........161

May the Road Rise to Meet You...............................163

INTRODUCTION

At this point in my life, at age 77, in 2017, I have been in the ministry for 57 years. The purpose for this book is to help people on the road of life. I thank God for this Pentecostal message of Acts 2:38, the oneness of God, holiness within, holiness with-out and separation from the world. I thank Him every day for this revelation. We can do all the above and to be saved we must. After we have obeyed Acts 2:38 and are really living for God, we still have to live in this life. We have to cope with this life. The Bible says, "He that endureth unto the end the same shall be saved." So the purpose of this book is to help Apostolic Jesus Name people on the road called Life.

In this book are lessons I have learned in life. Some of it is original, and some of it is not. I can't take credit for everything, but I wanted to put something together, by the help of God, that would help us cope with life and make heaven.

I read this somewhere, I do not remember when or where, but I liked it:

"Who am I? Why am I here? What should I do? What is my destiny? What does it all mean?" These are some questions we ask ourselves as we undertake life's journey. We are searching for meaning. As thinking people, we want to understand why we find ourselves on this road, and where the journey is taking us.

Will that place make us truly happy and fulfilled? If we could first know where we are, we could better judge what to do, and how to do it. We are wanderers, searching and striving for end and aim, for purpose and connection. In many respects life is an inward journey.

Life is indeed a journey from the cradle to the grave.
It is a journey of understanding one's self and God's will.

I do understand, as you read this book you may be young or old or in between. Different people will be at different places in life. I pray the lessons in this book will help us on this journey – called LIFE. It's like the song that Timothy Spell sings...

Day After Day

Day after day, that's what life is.
Live, work and play; that's what life is.

Someday we'll lay it all down.
We'll pick up a robe and a crown.
Yesterday lies in the past,
And only the good things are gonna last.
I'll bid this old world adieu
When my day-by-day journey is through.

REMEMBER

The lessons in this book

are only seed thoughts.

They are not in depth.

You will have to take it

and let it grow from there.

A couple of years ago, my oldest grandson, Drew, was interested in where the Mortons came from. So, he and I flew into Dallas, rented a car, and went down into West Texas in the Midland-Odessa area, way out in the country. We visited the old home place, but it was now many, many years later. There was nothing left at the old home place except for an old windmill. There used to be two houses and two windmills. Now there is just one old windmill, and it doesn't work.

As I stood there that day gazing at the old windmill, memory came by, and took me by the hand, back to when I lived there as just a boy. It was called the Hatchett farm because a man by the name of Earl Hatchett owned the place. We were share croppers. You can say this was the beginning of my journey, and I want to share with you some of the things that have helped me on this road called Life.

I stood there and thought about how my daddy and uncles used to plow those fields. We had hogs, chickens, horses, cows, and of course, rattlesnakes and dogs. That was home. I remembered the pond that used to be there and how I played there as a boy. As I was looking at the windmill and thinking these things over, unbeknown to me, my grandson Drew took a picture. Later, he had the picture printed on a canvas, and he wrote these words:

Memories

The memories, they visit me
Like an old sweet friend.
And yes, they remind me
How good God has been.

Even now, it is a desolate place. Drew said, "Papa, just to think, God brought you from this place to California and revealed the truth to you. Had that not happened, I may not have been in the truth today."

I was not born and raised in this Jesus Name, Acts 2:38, One God, Apostolic Way. So now it is many, many, many years later, and I have walked on this road of life and want to share with you in this book some of the things that have helped me on this journey.

Life teaches us much of which we are not aware.

Memories

The memories, they visit me
Like an old sweet friend.
And yes, they remind me
How good God has been.
~ Drew Morton

Lesson 1 – Reality

At our Donkey Rock Youth Camp in July of 2005, I was talking to someone. We were talking about all of the food that we eat at camp. Three big meals a day and then after service we eat again. We eat this way for at least six days and some of us get there early and make it seven or eight days. This person asked me, "Do you bring your scale to camp?"

I said, "No."

This person said, "When I get home I will not get on the scale for at least a week."

I said, "I am going home Friday, and I will get up Saturday morning, and I will step on the scale and face the reality."

The lesson here is too many times in life we don't want to face the reality of life, whatever that reality might be. Such as, "I don't want to look at the bills." "I don't want to talk to so and so about the problem we have." "I don't want to get on the scale." We have something to do, but we keep putting it off.

The word *reality* means the state or fact of being real or true. It also means actual existence, the true state of affairs. So we must learn this lesson on the journey of life - face reality and deal with it.

Now go get on the scale.

Lesson 2
Climber, Camper or Quitter

One time many years ago, I had a friend of mine named Howard Avery who owned a hand car wash in Fresno. I had my cars washed there for many years. He said to me, "Bro. Morton, in life you are one of three things: a climber, a camper or a quitter."

So what are we going to be in life? A climber, a camper or a quitter?

A climber is one who climbs or helps in climbing. The campers do not climb. They don't quit. They just camp. They make no progress. A quitter is one who quits, who gives up easily, and who is a defeatist.

Right now, do we know what we are? Are we a climber, a camper or a quitter?

We in Fresno live close to Yosemite National Park. I have gone to the Yosemite Valley and with binoculars watched as rock climbers scaled straight up the rock face of the mountain. It really is breathtaking watching the mountain climbers.

In life, we will never get out of that hole that we are in by camping or quitting. We have got to get up and climb!

There have been times in my life when things were out of my control. I felt like I was in a deep, dark hole, but by God's grace and help, I climbed out. I could not have gotten out if I had been a camper or a quitter.

I like the song that says, "I am climbing up the rough side of the mountain." Life is like a grindstone—it will either grind us down or polish us up. To be successful in life, we must have the right attitude; the attitude of a climber, not the attitude of a camper and not the attitude of a quitter.

We will never climb above our attitude. You may say as you read here today, "Bro. Morton, I feel like a failure." Remember, failure is the opportunity to begin again. So start climbing!

Attitude makes the difference.

Sometimes we look at a problem and say, "That problem is just too big for me. I can't do it." That is the attitude of a camper or a quitter. David, when he looked at Goliath, didn't say, "Goliath is too big for me." He looked at him with the attitude, "Goliath is a target too big to miss."

The Bible says in the book of Job that in the end, God blessed him with twice as much as he ever had. Do you know why God blessed him? Because he had the spirit of a climber - not a camper, not a quitter.

Remember, God is up to something when we are down to nothing.

In my ministry, I have watched as some have camped and some have quit. I have watched others as they have climbed. What are we going to do when we are down and out and depressed, or things are not going good? Are we going to just camp there? quit there? or climb out?

In II Corinthians 11:24, Paul tells us all that he went through. He was not a camper or a quitter. He was a climber!

One day my friend Howard said to me,

> *"Brother Morton, yard by yard anything is hard, but inch by inch anything is a cinch."*

So I say to you, "Keep climbing even if it is inch by inch!" That is better than being a camper or a quitter.

Keep that song in your heart, "I Am Climbing Up the Rough Side of the Mountain." Be a climber! Not a camper or a quitter.

P.S. Come on, by the help of God, you can do it!

Lesson 3
Against the Wind

In my house over the fireplace is a sculpture that the church bought me many years ago. It is big, it is heavy, and I really like it. It talks to me.

The sculpture is of a cowboy holding his hat so it will not blow off and he is leaning into the wind. The title of the sculpture is, "Against the Wind." Life is like that sometimes. We have to lean into the wind and hold on to our hat. Just keep walking and believing that a better day is coming.

Maybe the wind is blowing in your life right now, and you are having to hold your hat and lean into the wind. I say just keep walking. Everything is gonna to be alright.

Lesson 4
Are We Doing the Best We Can?

One time, while I was preaching in a certain city, the pastor was driving me around town. As we took a quiet side street, standing there on the street corner was an old well-dressed black gentleman. The pastor said, "I know that man. His name and my name and our initials are the same." The pastor rolled down his window and called the gentleman by name and said, "How you doin'?"

The old gentleman stood there for a few moments and stared off into space like he was thinking deeply. He finally answered, "<u>I am doing the best I can</u>." It was like he thought it all over, and he came to the conclusion that he was doing the best he could.

I never forgot that day because the encounter put something in me. I say to myself, "Vaughn Morton, are you doing the best you can in living for God?"

So I ask you today, are we doing the best we can in taking care of our relationship with God, our marriages, our families, our churches? So you can just use your imagination from here. Let's ask ourselves, "Are we doing the best we can?" If not, let's make a change and start giving our best.

Lesson 5
Doing What We Don't Want to Do

To every thing there is a season, and a time to every purpose under the heaven. (Ecclesiastes 3:1)

Better is the end of a thing than the beginning thereof: and the patient in spirit is better than the proud in spirit. (Ecclesiastes 7:8)

Whatsoever thy hand findeth to do, do it with thy might; for there is no work, nor device, nor knowledge, nor wisdom, in the grave, whither thou goest. (Ecclesiastes 9:10)

Our subject for this lesson is doing what we don't want to do, what we don't like to do, until something better comes along. Sometimes in life we say, "I do not want to do this any longer. I don't like doing this, but we have to learn to do it anyway until something better comes along......and it may never come along." We may have to do what we don't like to do for the rest of our lives.

You see, sometimes we are like David of old. He wanted to escape life. David said, "Oh that I had wings like a dove! for then would I fly away, and be at rest. Lo, then would I wander far off, and remain in the wilderness. I would hasten my escape from the windy storm and tempest." (Psalms 55:6-8).

It is like the words of the song we have already used, day after day that's what life is. A lot of people got up this morning not wanting to, but they did it anyway. It is called discipline. We have got to do what we don't want to do. We just do it anyway.

We may say, "I am not a morning person; I don't want to get up." We have got to get up anyway. A big part of life is doing what we don't want to do. Think of all the things in life that you have had to do and that you are doing right now, that you didn't want to do.

I am reminded of our youth camp that we have been doing for way over 30 years. Our youth camp is a place called Donkey Rock. Every year during the camp the sewer line valve has to be turned and changed. No one really wants to do it.

One day I thought about it, and I said, "That valve needs to be turned." You have to understand it is not a clean job. It is not a good smelling job, and you have to put your hand in water that you don't really want to put your hand in. I thought, "That valve needs to be changed." I went to where the valve was, took off the lid and reached down into the muck. A little boy about 8 years old was standing there watching me. One of the lady counselors walked by, looked, smelled and said "WOO!" then walked on. The small boy standing there had some wisdom. As he walked away I heard him say, "<u>Sometimes a man has gotta do what a man has gotta do</u>."

I did not want to do it, but it needed to be done; so I did it anyway. We read in the Bible a lot of people had to do what they didn't want to do, but they did it anyway.

Remember we are talking about doing what we don't want to do until something better comes along. In life there must be discipline. I want to tell you about some things in life that I have done that I didn't want to do.

I was born and raised in my formative years in West Texas. We farmed way out in the country. We had no electric lights, no running water (we got our water from a windmill), and no inside toilet. We were poor folks doing the best we could. On a farm like that there are a lot of things to do that you don't want to do. I watched my daddy do it. In other words, he did it anyway.

Right after World War II we moved to California. In those days in California a lot of the kids went to the fields to work. I used to go with my Grandpa Stanifer to cut grapes. Cutting grapes was a hot and dirty job. I didn't want to, but I did it anyway. As a kid, during the summer, I worked in the fruit to make a little money. I worked to buy some Levis and have some spending money. One of the things I really didn't like was picking blackberries, but I got up early every morning before daylight and rode my bicycle to the field and did it anyway. One morning before sunrise, I got up, went to work, fell in the dark and broke a rib. I still went to work anyway!

I remember getting a good job one summer, turning raisin trays for 75 cents an hour. In those days we just learned, although we didn't like it, to keep doing what we had to do until something better came along. You know a good policy to live by is, "Don't quit a job until you get another one."

As a teenager, I didn't know anything about Pentecost, but I got acquainted with the church, repented, got the Holy Ghost, got baptized in Jesus Name. I obeyed Acts 2:38.

I remember going to high school and working at a dry cleaners. I wasn't lazy, but I hated the job. Now this is good for you young preachers.... As a teenager, God was dealing with me about the ministry. I didn't go around telling people, but I felt my call to preach. I wanted to preach, and I didn't want to work at the cleaners; but I did it anyway. I didn't want to unload boxcars of hardwood floors, but I did it anyway. I will never forget when I got a job for $1.55 an hour, working at a turkey processing plant in the summer.

To tell you the truth, I didn't like going to school at all! But I never quit, and I graduated from the twelfth grade. I was wanting to preach. I worked at a Texaco station, and in those days they called them filling stations. We put in gas, checked the oil and the water, washed the windows, and checked the air. Gas was about 20 cents a gallon. Remember, I was a young preacher; but I listened to my pastor, and I waited on my ministry. I got a job working in construction and installing septic systems and pumping septic tanks. Go learn what that means.....

I had just graduated from high school, and somebody asked my pastor if I could preach them a revival. With my pastor's blessing, I did, and that first revival lasted four weeks. Now I was doing what I liked! From there, with my pastor's blessing, and not until, I went into the ministry, finally doing what I wanted to do. Remember, I kept doing all those other things until something better came along. I will close by saying, just keep on keeping on 'til something better comes along.

Lesson 6
Dealing With a Problem

If we have a problem, we need to take care of it as soon as we can. The word *problem* means unsettled questions, a source of perplexity or distress, a matter or situation regarded as unwelcome or harmful and needing to be dealt with and overcome.

There is a difference between having a problem and being a problem. There was a time many, many years ago when I felt like a brother in the Lord had a problem with me for some reason. It bothered me. I gave him a call and I asked, "Brother, have I offended you, or is there a problem between you and me?" He said, "No." Then about three hours later he called me back and said, "Brother Morton, I was not honest with you. I do have a problem. You were honest enough to call me and ask me. I wasn't honest with you. It bothers me, and so I am calling you back to fix it......" We had a good discussion, and it ended well. This good man had a problem. He got honest with himself and said, "I am going to fix this," and he did.

We need to be honest about our problem; whatever it might be. He fixed the problem, and I am sure he felt better in his heart. I know I felt better. It gave me a greater respect for this man.

Sometimes we are asked the question, "Is everything alright?" and we say, "Yes!" and things are not alright. We need to be honest and lay it all out.

*If we have a problem
we need to just deal with it.*

For every problem under the sun
There is a solution or there is none,
If there is one try to find it,
If there is none never mind it.

How true this is! We must not drive ourselves crazy trying to find an answer when there is none.

Lesson 7
We Can't Un-ring a Bell

We all know the story, the tragic story of David and his sin, and how he failed God. The man of God, Nathan, came to him and said, "Thou art the man." David's heart smote him and his conviction led him to his prayer of repentance as recorded in Psalm 51. As David looked back on his life, he no doubt wished that he had never rung that bell. We need to be careful with what we say and what actions we take because many times, once we ring that bell, we can never un-ring it. I suppose we can all look back on our life and say, "I wish I hadn't said that or done that." We wish we could go back and un-ring the bell, but we can't. We must proceed in life on this journey with caution.

P.S. By the way, you can't unscramble eggs either...

I want to draw special attention to the next three lessons because they can be sensitive. Sad to say, broken homes are among us. **We have got to face this reality of life.** I want to let parents, children, and young people know God is still in control no matter life's circumstances.

I have asked Sis. Teresa Wodoslawsky and my son, Nathan, to write the feelings of their hearts regarding living, surviving, and overcoming life in a broken home. They both are living successful and victorious lives in their marriages, families, and ministries.

This is not taking a doctrinal stand. **These are lessons to help those who are working through the process of a broken home.** Fifty years later, I can say for myself, "God's grace is sufficient."

Lesson 8
Tragedy of a Broken Home
by Elder Vaughn Morton

On this road called Life, and in this day that we are living in, there is something I want to talk about. We do not enjoy this subject, but we must face the reality that is among us. It is the **tragedy of a broken home**. If you have never experienced it, I pray this is one encounter in life that you will never go through. If you have gone through it or if you are going through it, may this lesson be a help to you. Maybe you could use this lesson to help a loved one or a friend. I have asked my son, Bro. Nathan Morton and Sis. Teresa Wodoslawsky to contribute to this lesson because in younger years as children and young people they faced this unpleasant experience. They have been there and done that. They came out of it, by the help of God, victorious and are living for God today. By God's grace, you can do it too.

Our lesson is the tragedy of a broken home. Now I know that this subject hurts, but I do not mean to hurt any heart. You see, in the beginning, all was well in the home of Adam and Eve, and then the devil came to visit that home. In John 10:10, "THE THIEF COMETH NOT, BUT FOR TO STEAL, AND TO KILL, AND TO DESTROY." We know how Adam and Eve fell into sin. Because of sin, homes can be broken. I know that some of us may have some inner feelings in our hearts because of a broken home or marriage. Remember, tears that fall on the outside quickly go away, but tears that fall on the inside stay and stay and stay. Crying on the inside can be a silent sorrow. We can't get out of this life without scars. Jesus didn't. He had scars in His hands, feet, and heart.

Isaiah 53 says, He was despised, rejected, a man of sorrows and acquainted with grief. He was wounded, oppressed and afflicted. Yet He opened not his mouth. When He did open His mouth He said, "Father, forgive them." He gave up His right to retaliate or to take vengeance or to get even. Some things in life we can't fix. We just have to leave it with God. We must not let a root of bitterness spring up in our hearts.

Every home has its battles. Some just know how to be more private about it than others. We that are from a broken situation must not hide the hurt in our heart, but we must break before God. A family is where hearts understand each other. It should be side by side at the altar of love.

One man said, "Tragedy came to me and I said, 'What does tragedy want with me?' A voice said, 'She has come to show you the earth and its sorrows. For he who has not looked on sorrow will never see joy.'" It has been well said that sorrow can purify the heart or make it bitter. We alone must decide which it will be.

I Corinthians 7 says, "They that marry shall have trouble in the flesh." Two minds, two wills, two ways, two sets of feelings, and two wants. A house is built by human hands. A home is built by human hearts, two hearts that are together, husband and wife. Husband, wife, and children form the world's greatest team. Whether that team wins or loses depends largely upon whether that husband and wife practice human love in the home.

We must not trade our families for anything – money, friends, job, play things, business, another woman, or another man. One of the most important things a father and mother can do for their children is to love each other. You that want to get married had better make sure that it is someone of like faith and conviction.

A real home is a happy home, yet there is no perfect home. Every home has its "deals." It has to be worked at all the time. It is our life's work, day after day. A real home has understanding, wisdom, courtesy, thoughtfulness, helpfulness, responsibility, work, play, security, humor, loyalty, faith, hope, laughter, sympathy, honest and open discussions, a place of refuge, a place of prayer and the Word of God, the Bible, and church-going. Yet, at times, there will be tears and sorrow.

To build a house is one thing, but to make it a home is quite another. A home or family should be a place that our children would be proud to come back to, a place they can always call home. A boy or a girl will learn how to be a man or a woman by watching their father and mother.

Oh yes, the home is dear to the heart of God. Woe

be to the person that is the cause of a broken home or marriage. Woe be to the man or woman that puts scars on the heart of another. Woe be to the person that puts scars on the heart of a child. The word of God says, "But whoso shall offend one of these little ones which believe in me, it were better for him that a millstone were hanged about his neck, and *that* he were drowned in the depth of the sea." (Matthew 18:6) Woe be to the man that goes after another man's wife. Woe be to the woman that goes after another woman's husband. A person that will break up their home or another person's home is selfish and self-centered. They will suffer for it.

What are you doing to your home? Your children and your childrens' children will suffer for years to come. Some husbands and wives say, "We are staying together just for the children's sake. We don't love each other." May I say, "Your children are living in a broken home. You need to get your hearts together. You need to rededicate to each other." Oh! The tragedy of a broken home. The song says,

<blockquote>
Bind us together, Lord
Bind us together
With cords that cannot be broken,
Bind us together, Lord
Bind us together, Lord
Bind us together in love.
</blockquote>

I am reminded of a song that Pastor Wayne Lawhorn wrote and sings.

IT TAKES GOD TO MAKE A HOME

When I think of the blessings of the Lord
God's marvelous grace and so much more
He's smiled on me, he's been good to me and my family

I thank God for my family,
But a wife and a child,
Doesn't make a home
So many live together,
But they're always alone
It takes God to make a home

There are those who'll never know what a home really is
Children raised in a heated rage,
not knowing what true love is
It's oh so sad that Mom and Dad chose to live this way
If they could only see what God has purposed for every family

You've touched my home, my wife and kids
Given me a place to live, all I need, ever comes from you
So many times I never gave it a thought
You gave me a home that can't be bought
Millions would love to exchange.

ONE STORY FROM THE DIVIDE
By Nathan Morton

So here we are, faced with discussing something so very sad and delicate as divorce. Sadly, divorce is now very commonplace, even among Apostolics. Yet, I'm glad I'm in a place that I can talk about it without bitterness, angst and no healing. And I'm in that place because my parents, with all of the irresolvable differences between them, helped me get there, along with the unfailing, pursuing grace of God. First let me say - Dad and Mom, I love you both very, very much. This isn't stringing dirty family laundry out for all to see. I'm way beyond that, and you two are fine with me, and with my family, so it's all good. This is simply my attempt to help some who may need a little assistance to get on down the road of life rather than be stalled on the side by a broken family.

There is no way here to cover every issue and every particular situation. There's a lot of ground I'm not covering here due to people's privacy, and to limited space. But there's **good news** in all of the pain that everyone in any of these situations suffers at the divide – it does not have to be the end of the world! I'm writing this as a happy, well-adjusted, Apostolic family man. Myself married for 28 years at the time of this writing, and enjoying a very normal, healthy family of my own. I am not at all downplaying the devastation of divorce, but neither am I faking my own normality. God is good in all circumstances, and that includes the rending of a family. **Divorce is not greater than God's ability to bring wholeness.**

And I am very happy to report that both of my parents, though never getting their marriage back together, are living for God and being wonderful parents and grandparents. I can't explain it all, just this; when we decide that the wrecked aftermath of divorce will not be our final destination, moving on to healing and a great family life is possible. And that means you too. To us kids of divorce, very likely, it's a powerful help to our parents when they see us grow greater than the divorce.

I'm not an authority on divorce, just a voice among many on this issue. Here, I'm not holding forth any doctrinal position; I'm not casting judgment on anyone, I'm not rubbing anyone's nose in their problems. I am also very aware every divorce has its own unique personality, pain and fallout, and I am not equipped with all the answers to every situation.

For our family, the split happened at the time I was 17 months old. I don't know that there is such a thing as a good divorce. Maybe less destructive than others, but not good. I grew up in a single parent home with my mother. My father was very much involved, but the day to day was with mom, and she gave my brother and I a great home life.

My problems with the split didn't start until I was a teenager. I would seesaw back and forth between resenting my dad, then my mom – then over here, then over there, why did she, why did he, on and on, blah, blah, blah. The biggest struggle? "Why am I having to deal with all of this because my parents couldn't get their act together? They pull their stunt and then leave me to deal with it. Thanks a lot!" I was bitter, and allowing the pain of the split to eat me up. My parents were actually doing a good job, but as a teenager, one sees things through a distorted lens.

Now, I need to pause here a moment to say something, and this is important – **thank God for the church!** Divorced parent, immerse yourself and your kids in the church family! The friendships, the Spirit of God filling in all the gaps, the preaching, the busyness of wholesome, purposeful activity – it is good medicine that heals enough to no longer need the medicine!

Very long story short – God intervened, powerfully, completely. Sitting in a youth conference in Bakersfield, California, the preacher, Bro. James Kilgore, was preaching to us young people about finding our place in the will of God. Then there seemed to come on him a strong unction of the Spirit as he exclaimed forcefully, "There's a young person tonight in this service, and you are going to miss God's will for your life if you can't get over your bitterness toward the authority and circumstances in your life!" Bam! Pretty clear! He's talking right to me. God stuck His finger in my chest to make me face some decisions that were mine alone to make.

I don't have enough space here to explain what happened in that service. God shook me to my depths with this: the divorce is your parents' cross to bear, but what are *you* going to do, Nathan? You gonna keep living there, churning it up? You gonna keep excusing your own ugly attitude because of someone else's situation? You gonna keep wallowing in the "unfairness" of it? Or are you gonna rise above it and march on to your future, and never let this cripple you again? Because it is crippling you. And the crippling is not your parents' fault, it's yours. Get over it and get on with your life!

I literally spent several hours praying, and replaying what life had been and what it would be if I didn't move on. I spent hours after that talking with my dad; and later on with my mom. I came to myself, and found the release I needed. I was free. I decided not to wear the label and accept the excuses, not to drink the Kool-Aid that I would be disabled emotionally, functionally, relationally. Sure, I'm probably a little dented maybe, but running fine.

Their divorce, while permanently part of my story, was no longer the only part of my story, nor the biggest part of my story. I was now the author of the rest of my story. I didn't have to have all the answers. I didn't have to carry that dead carcass around with me. I didn't have to judge who was more wrong and who was more right. I just had to take care of my own life, and God put before me wonderful opportunities. I figured it out – that I didn't really have to have it all figured out.

A few things here I believe to be important. First, to the parents in the divorce. Great news! The kids are resilient! They're not as fragile as you think! Don't make them so by fretting, hand wringing angst and overmuch psychoanalyzing. I don't mean they don't need help, even special consideration; sure, their world is crashing down, and there will be painful wreckage. But it won't necessarily be the cause of them wrecking their own life. Not only did I make it through, but I have pastored for twenty years, and helped many families, especially the kids, navigate the violent storms of divorce – and for the most part they make it! The seas will calm, the sun will break through, they will find a safe harbor. I hate to use a negative comparison, but I can count off plenty of kids from unbroken homes who were disasters, so I feel safe to say a divorce is not a predictor of wholesale destruction of the kids. Parents, if you go at this with a we're-hurting-but-we're-gonna-be-all-right attitude, that will go far toward fortifying the kids' resilience.

Also parents, you're gonna have to cut the kids some slack in some areas. The holidays, vacations, graduations, weddings, family reunions, all kinds of other such considerations – that time and those events are now divided in half between you parents, so don't go all pouty if the kids can't spend as much time or a certain day with you, or don't always know how to handle a certain dynamic. Be gracious and selfless, make it easy on them to deal with these things. You won't win in the long run trying to demand.

Those kids are gonna need time and understanding to work through their own process. They don't have the maturity of an adult. They may act out, or close in or go through all sorts of tumults in the process. Be understanding, be patient. I don't mean put up with ugly disrespect, but on the other hand some longsuffering will be required.

Further parents, never, never, never, never use those kids as game pieces to score against your ex! Did I say never? Trying to use the kids as tools to prove your own points, strike back against your ex, whatever, this is a huge mistake! Those kids will probably discern someday if you used them thus, and the resentment will be huge! And they may not share with you all the negative feelings toward your ex. You wouldn't serve them poison, do not do so with their spirits either. Or, they may feel too much bitterness toward one parent – don't feed that beast! It'll turn on you someday if you do.

Now, us kids of the divorce. You may be broken now,

but do not believe that you have to remain broken! Don't believe you now have a right to remain bitter, the right to behave badly. You may be weak now, but don't remain weak and accept that you're off the hook for your own faults because your parents threw you unwillingly into their mess. You're better than that! Why should their life define your own? You and hopefully God are the authors of your story – don't hand the pen to anyone else!

Do the best you can with your parents. Fortunately for me, my parents, while they couldn't make the spouse thing work, did make the parent thing work. I know for some of you, that's not the case. Maybe one or both of your parents didn't do right by you in the divorce or a remarriage, but listen, there are other good people around you who can take up that slack. Yes, they are there, and God will help you find them. Don't fixate on the divorce so much that you lose sight of what else is right in your life – and *who* else is right in your life.

There's a song by Matthew West entitled "Forgiveness." One line of the lyrics goes like this, "*So let it go and be amazed, by what you see through eyes of grace, the prisoner that it really frees - is you.*"

It's time to let it go.

There's a great big world out there filled with wonderful things and wonderful relationships. Get out there and live it! Stop staying shut up in that prison of divorce. Move away from the divide.

BEAUTY FOR ASHES
By Teresa Wodoslawsky

First, I want to thank God. **He has made the difference in my life**. Second, in my teenage years, my 20's and my 30's, I did not have the perspective that I now have regarding divorce and growing up in a broken home. Divorce is a very difficult thing and hard for a young child or teenager to comprehend or work through.

My parents were divorced before I could even walk. I do not have any memory of them together. For me life has always been this way. In my early childhood years, I just remember an intense desire to "make everyone happy." Both sides! I love my mom and I love my dad. In my teenage years, I struggled with, "Why can't my life or my family be like everyone elses? I want a mom and a dad not a mom and step-dad and a dad and step-mom!"

I was not raised Apostolic, but God miraculously changed my life at age 12 when I received the revelation of the oneness of God, was baptized in Jesus name and received the Holy Ghost. Then at age 16, God blessed me by allowing Pastor and Sis. Hale to come into my life. Their guidance, prayer and countless hours in their home helped me to be successful as a young person living for God. Sis. Hale would pick me up for early morning prayer and we would go to the church together. Those times are still precious memories of my life. I cannot adequately express my gratefulness to her for allowing me to step in during her private time of prayer with the

Almighty. Those prayer meetings shaped me and molded me. My prayer life that grew out of those encounters would carry me through dark times of emptiness and feelings of incompleteness as a child of divorce. Pastor Hale's compassion, prayer, anointed preaching and determination are what guided me through the difficult teenage years. To them, I am forever grateful and thankful.

In my young adult years, I just wanted to fit in to a family and feel like I belonged. I thought that feeling would be fulfilled in my marriage to my wonderful husband. My marriage did not fulfill the emptiness and incompleteness inside. I can take you to the exact place where God began dealing with me. It was the living room floor of our second apartment, about six months into our marriage. It was there while praying that I realized I had not let God in the secret parts of my life. I had not let God into the emptiness of my deepest desires. I had successfully covered the emptiness with laughter, smiles, happiness and fun times. **God knew where I was, and He knew when I was ready to be changed.** That encounter in the floor of my living room was just the very beginning. God would take me on a journey of healing and wholeness step by step and situation by situation. God is gentle, kind, patient and merciful.

God has always placed people in my life that have helped me. Every preacher who preached the anointed Word of God helped me along my journey. Every message that taught me God is sufficient, all powerful, all knowing! I was just one in the crowd of many, but those messages and the presence of God are what guided me and helped me.

One of my last epiphanies came when I was about thirty-five years old. It was then that I truly felt released, whole, victorious and unphased by being raised in a divorced home. Thirty-five! The effects of divorce do not just disappear on their own, neither does God want us to ignore or bury the hurt, but He wants to heal. Remember this is my story and your story will most likely be vastly different. The details are not that important to tell.

God is able! He is the same yesterday, today and forever! He is big enough, strong enough, loving enough, caring enough to carry you through whatever your situation may be. Our lives are IN God's hands and He is very capable of taking care of us. The only factor that changes is us! If we submit to God, give ALL to God, trust God with EVERYTHING and all parts of our lives... He is the ONE that makes the difference.

My wholeness and completeness came through time, piece by piece, as God brought people, situations, and thoughts into my life. God brought me help in the time of my trouble. Yes, I may not have started in the game of Life with the best set of odds, but it doesn't matter! It is God who makes me a WINNER!

What advice would I give to another young person or adult struggling through a life of brokenness? Don't get bitter! Develop the closest possible relationship with Jesus Christ and trust HIM with everything! If your life is truly in God's hands – you too will be victorious.

The Spirit of the Lord GOD is upon me; because the LORD hath anointed me to preach good tidings unto the meek; he hath sent me to <u>bind up the brokenhearted</u>, to proclaim <u>liberty to the captives</u>, and the opening of the prison to them that are bound; To proclaim the acceptable *year of the LORD, and the day of vengeance of our God; to <u>comfort all that mourn</u>; To appoint unto them that mourn in Zion, to give unto them <u>beauty for ashes</u>, the <u>oil of joy for mourning</u>, the <u>garment of praise for the spirit of heaviness</u>; that they might be called trees of righteousness, the planting of the LORD, that <u>he might be glorified</u>.* (Isaiah 61:1-3)

Lesson 9
We Can't Allow the Past to Decide Our Future

*"Courage is being scared to death,
but saddling up anyway, and riding on."*

Brethren, I count not myself to have apprehended: but this one thing I do, forgetting those things which are behind, and reaching forth unto those things which are before, I press toward the mark for the prize of the high calling of God in Christ Jesus. (Philippians 3:13-14)

Remember, David failed God. We can read his prayer of repentance in Psalm 51. One thing David did not do is allow the past to decide his future. No matter what has happened in our past, let us not live there and wallow there. Let's have faith in God and move on to the future because there is no living in the past. There is no life in the past and there is no future in the past.

Let's ask ourselves this question "Am I going to be a shadow for the past or an outline of the future?" It takes courage to move on. Like the old cowboy said,

"Courage is being scared to death, but saddling up anyway, and riding on."

Lesson 10
The Game Is Only Half Over

In 1929 Georgia Tech University played the University of California in the Rose Bowl. In the game, a player from the California team recovered a fumble but he became confused and ran the wrong way. A teammate tackled him just before he would have scored a touchdown against his own team.

At halftime all of the players went into the dressing room and sat down, wondering what the coach would say. This young man sat by himself and put a towel over his head and cried. When the team was ready to go back onto the field for the second half, the coach stunned the team by telling the young man, "You will be playing again in the second half."

The young man said, "Coach, I can't do it. I have ruined you. I have disgraced the University of California, and I can't face the crowd in the stadium again." Then the coach put his hand on the young man's shoulder and said, "Son, get up and go back in! <u>The game is only half over!</u>"

I don't know where you might be in life right now. It could be you are hurting because of a past failure or mistake. You are alive. You are reading this book, and life is not over. It is time to get back in the game of life and prove yourself a winner. No failure need be final.

Lesson 11
God Doesn't Expect Us to Fix Everything

I read a little story one time by a man named Charlie W. Shedd. I thought the story was very good. The story is titled "*God Doesn't Expect us To Do Everything.*" But I would like to change the title to "*God Doesn't Expect Us To Fix Everything.*" The story goes like this:

Grandpa was working on his backyard gate, when his young grandson appeared. He paused a while as small boys will, then he asked, "Whacha doing grandpa?"

To which the aged sage replied, "Son, there are five kinds of broken things in this life."

"Number one, there is the kind which, when they are broken, can never be fixed. Number two, there are the kind that will fix themselves if you leave them alone. Number three, there are also the kind which are none of my business, and someone else has got to fix them.

Number four, there are the kind which, when they are broken, you should never worry about them; only God can fix them. Number five, there are the kind that I have to fix. That is what I am doing. I am fixing this old gate, because if I don't fix it, it will never get fixed."

So God doesn't expect us to fix everything. We need to pray that God would give us wisdom and discernment to know what to fix and what not to fix.

Lesson 12
God, It's in Your Hands

In making our way through life we have to learn to commit things to God. One day when I was pastoring at Truth Tabernacle in Fresno, California (I pastored there for 41 ½ years), as my custom was, I was praying in the church in the morning. I really, really had something on my mind and on my heart that needed earnest prayer and God's attention. As I was praying, walking back and forth by the altar, I said "Oh God. Oh God. This is in Your hands. Your will be done. God, I want Your will, Your way, Your time." It seemed to me that the spirit of the Lord came to me, or maybe it was just inspiration, but it came to me. It really helped me, and that was....

*What better hands could it be in
than the hands of God?*

The scripture came to me, "*Casting all your care upon him; for he careth for you.*" (I Peter 5:7) In other words, just simply put it in the hands of God. There was a peace and tranquility that came to me at that moment. It came when I felt like I really, really did commit it to God and that He would bring it to pass in His will, His time and His way. This is just a simple lesson that happened to me in life that has been a real blessing to me for many years.

Just put it in the hands of God.

Just Let It Unfold

It's only a tiny rosebud,
A flower of God's design,
But I cannot unfold the petals
With these clumsy hands of mine.

The secret of unfolding flowers
Is not known to such as I.
The flower that opens so sweetly
Would in my hands fade and die.

If I cannot unfold a rose bud,
This flower of God's design,
Then how can I think I have wisdom
To unfold this life of mine.

So I'll trust in Him for His leading
Each moment of every day,
I'll look to Him for His guidance
Each step of the pilgrim way.

> For the pathway that lies before me,
> My heavenly Father knows.
> I'll trust Him to unfold the moments
> Just as He unfolds the rose.
> ~ Author Unknown

Don't try to take it out of His hands. Let Him make the decision. The Bible says, "...and it came to pass..." When it comes to pass, accept it as the will of God. God's decisions are the best. Sometimes God has a process for us to go through to get to the right answer.

And we know that all things work together for good to them that love God, to them who are the called according to his purpose. (Romans 8:28)

The Bible is such a wonderful book. Thank God for the Bible. Because of it we can see how God works. We can see how He has worked in the lives of other people. When they were going through it, they did not know the end, but God was working. Everything was fitting into His plan. Joseph wanted to be free, but God wanted him in jail. Remember the story of Elijah who wanted to die, but God wanted him to live. Life is not always clear, but God can guide us with His eye.

Lesson 13
God's Time

Ecclesiastes 8:5 states: "... a wise man's heart discerneth both time and judgment." Another way to say it is, "A wise man knows in his heart the right time and method for action." Also, Ecclesiastes 8:6 states: "Because to every purpose there is a time and judgement." In other words, there is a proper time and procedure for everything. For every purpose and matter has its right time. Let me close this little thought by saying, there is a time and place for everything. Timing is so very important.

God's Will, God's Way, God's Time

Lesson 14
Heavy Sack

On this road called Life, I had a friend, a good friend. His name was Howard Avery. He owned a hand car wash and he washed my car for many years before he passed. He was full of good little thoughts. I remember one time he told me about digging potatoes. Of course, we called them "taters." He said that his daddy taught him a lesson. "Howard, do you want money? And lots of it?" Howard said, "Yeah, daddy!"

"You see that long row of taters," he said, "I want to tell you something, Son. The more money you want, you have got to have a heavy sack. In other words, the more taters you dig up and the heavier your sack gets, the more money you are going to have. Diggin' up them taters is like picking up money, go to work, Son."

A lot of people are wanting more, but they are not

willing to tow the heavy sack. Now, you can apply this to a whole lot of things in life. Life is a long row with a lot of taters to dig up, but it will be worth it all when you get to the other end of the row. Your sack will be full and heavy. You don't get something for nothing. So go dig taters.

Lesson 15
The Cowboy

I saw a picture once. The cowboy was under his horse in the storm. The horse had his head down and the rain was falling and the wind was blowing. The picture states, "Sometimes in life you just got to hunker down and wait for the storm to pass."

*I say hunker down and pray
till the storm passes!*

Lesson 16
Hurry Up, Sun Up

I saw a picture in Brother Rick Bray's office. I am trying to remember it the best I can. There was snow on the ground and everything looked dark and gloomy. The cowboy is hunkered down by a small fire. His horse was standing nearby. The man is holding his dog in his arms. It looked like the horse was depressed, the dog was depressed, and the cowboy was depressed. The caption on the picture is "Hurry Up, Sun Up."

That is the way it can be in life sometimes. It is cold. It is dark. It is gloomy, and it is depressing. We are just like the old cowboy, sitting there waiting for the sun to come up. The scripture says in Acts 27, Paul was in a storm out at sea and verse 29 says that they "wished for the day." Maybe today you are wishing for the day and you are saying, "Hurry up, Sun up."

Hey, let me tell you, the Sun IS going to shine again. Just hold on.

Lesson 17
The Mulligrubs

Sometimes in life we can get into the mulligrubs. Mulligrubs means "a despondent, sullen or ill-tempered mood." When we are in that type of mood, we can be turned inward. We are not doing ourselves or others any good.

This is just a little thought to help us out of the mulligrubs. To get our minds off of us and to be a blessing, get involved in the lives of others. We need to go find somebody to witness to, to share God's goodness. Invite them to church. Teach them a home Bible study. Spend time with them. Take them out for a meal. Invite them over to your house. There is nothing like the joy of soul winning!

You get such a joy when you witness to somebody and see that person repent, get baptized in Jesus name, and receive the Holy Ghost. Oh! The blessing in our church when new people come in, new faces, new voices, new blood, new testimonies. Watching them grow in God saves them and blesses us. We won't have time to be down in the dumps. The Bible does teach evangelism, winning the lost, witnessing, and giving of ourselves to others. Now go win a soul and get out of the mulligrubs!

Lesson 18
Joy! Joy! Joy!

On this road called Life, as we journey along, we have to be strong. Nehemiah 8:10 says, "The joy of the Lord is our strength." If that is true, and we know that it is, then we have to have a continuous renewing of joy. Psalms 16:11 tells us, "In His presence is fullness of joy." To have the strength that we need for this journey, we have to spend time in His presence worshipping, praying, and reading His word.

Remember what David said, "Restore unto me the joy of thy salvation." (Psalms 51:12) In other words, he was saying, "I need a revival of joy." Joy means "to be glad, merry, cheerful and happy." Acts 13:52 tells us that the disciples were filled with joy. It is important, very important, for us to be full, completely full, of the joy of the Lord. Remember, it is our strength. David said in Psalms 43:4, that God was his exceeding joy.

On this road called Life, there will be tears. Remember, Psalm 126:5 says, "They that sow in tears shall reap in joy." It also says in Psalms 30:5, "Weeping may endure for a night, but joy cometh in the morning." We must have faith that our tears will be turned into joy. We will have strength to journey on.

We can get so weighed down with life, just everyday life and stuff, that we can let it rob us of the joy of the Lord. When that is gone, our strength is gone, and the devil can take advantage of us. Isaiah 61 tells us, "He will give us the oil of joy for mourning and the garment of praise for the spirit of heaviness."

It is also important that we share our joy with others. I like the song that says "I've got the joy bells ringing, ring, ring, ringing, ring, ring, ringing, way down deep in my soul." There is nothing like joy juice. There is much in the Bible about the joy of the Lord. This is just a seed thought to remind us that the joy of the Lord is our strength. Joy! Joy! Joy! Let's journey on in the strength of the Lord.

Lesson 19
If You Are Not Part of the Problem

Here is another little thought that will keep us out of trouble on the road of life. We certainly want to stay out of trouble. If there is a problem and we are not part of the problem, or we are not part of the solution, then stay out of it. In other words, we need to learn to mind our own business. The Bible does talk about people being busybodies in other people's matters. Proverbs 26:17 states, "He that passeth by, and meddleth with strife, belonging not to him, is like one that taketh a dog by the ears." One commentary said, getting involved in an argument that is none of our business, is like going down the street and grabbing a dog by the ears – especially if it is a pit bull. We had better leave it alone! Some problems can turn into a pit bull.

"It is an honour for a man to cease from strife: but every fool will be meddling." (Proverbs 20:3) Meddling means to stick your nose where it doesn't belong. That's a good way to get a bloody nose.

I said all of that to say this. If we are not part of the problem and we are not part of the solution, then stay out of it, leave it alone, don't meddle and don't grab that dog by the ears. This little lesson can keep us out of a lot of trouble.

Lesson 20
Let Me Alone

And they went into Capernaum; and straightway on the sabbath day he entered into the synagogue, and taught. And they were astonished at his doctrine: for he taught them as one that had authority, and not as the scribes. And there was in their synagogue a man with an unclean spirit; and he cried out, Saying, **Let us alone**; *what have we to do with thee, thou Jesus of Nazareth? art thou come to destroy us? I know thee who thou art, the Holy One of God. And Jesus rebuked him, saying, Hold thy peace, and come out of him. And when the unclean spirit had torn him, and cried with a loud voice, he came out of him. And they were all amazed, insomuch that they questioned among themselves,*

saying, What thing is this? what new doctrine is this? for with authority commandeth he even the unclean spirits, and they do obey him. (Mark 1:21-27)

The unclean (foul) spirit cried out saying, "Let us alone!" The man with the unclean foul spirit was really saying, "LET ME ALONE!" As we pass through life, on our way to heaven we must not have the attitude of "LET ME ALONE!" In my years of pastoring, every so often you come to someone like that, "LET ME ALONE!" When we have that attitude, we can't be helped. The attitude of let me alone is a foul spirit. It is not good, and when children see a parent with that attitude, they can take on the same spirit of mama or daddy. We must be open to the man of God in our life. In Exodus 14:11-12, the people said to Moses, "Let us alone." We that are preachers or ministers must also be approachable by our elders.

And he gave some, apostles; and some, prophets; and some, evangelists; and some, pastors and teachers; For the perfecting of the saints, for the work of the ministry, for the edifying of the body of Christ: Till we all come in the unity of the faith, and of the knowledge of the Son of God, unto a perfect man, unto the measure of the stature of the fulness of Christ: (Ephesians 4:11-13)

This is a spirit that has been in the world as long as man has been in sin, but we as Apostolics must never take on the spirit of "LET ME ALONE!" Some people will not allow their pastor to pastor them. Blessed is the person who is submitted to the spiritual authority in their life.

Lesson 21
Me, Myself and I

As we make this journey of life we have to learn to cope with ourselves. Self, self, self; we are our own worst enemy – not the devil, not the world, not someone else, but self.

Alexander the Great

Alexander the Great was raised with a sense of destiny. At 20, he inherited the throne from his father. He then set out with 35,000 troops to conquer whatever he could. In the next 11 years, he marched more than 11,000 miles and never lost a battle. He was adored by his troops. But by 324 B.C. Alexander's own power became too intoxicating. He withdrew from the soldier's life and began drinking heavily.

He was in Babylon with his army in 323 B.C., preparing for his next campaign, and got into a drinking contest at a banquet. He is believed to have gulped down at least six quarts of wine. The next day, he was sick and caught cold, but continued to issue orders from his bed. Within ten days of his drinking feast, the conqueror was dead, having conquered everything but himself.

The meaning of the word self: personal interest, inbred, arrogant, self-centered, personal vanity, pride, an exaggerated estimate of one's own importance, self-willed, governed by one's own will, not yielding to the wishes of others.

The words "self" and "self-willed" can be found in the Bible. Self says, "It is me, myself and I." Self says, "It is all about me. Me and myself are the most important."

- Self is never wrong; and when it is, it was someone else's fault
- Self has to be at the forefront
- Self refuses to submit to authority
- Self refuses to acknowledge God–given authority
- Self is easily offended
- Self is blind to its own faults – but has x-ray vision when it comes to fault finding in others
- Self is critical about everything and everybody except, of course, self
- Self refuses to give unless it benefits self
- Self says, "What's in it for me?"
- Self has its life planned out, and nobody, including God, is going to interrupt its schedule
- Self loves the thrill of victory for self and is willing to see others suffer in order to attain it
- Self professes to love God when it is convenient for self

We must call self what it really is, that it is...selfish. Remember Alexander the Great conquered everything but himself. To be saved we must conquer our self. One man put it this way, "I have had just about all I can take of myself!"

Lesson 22
Tree Bent Out of Shape

At a place that we call "Donkey Rock", 6,000 feet above sea level, about two and a half hours from Fresno, up in the Sierra Mountains, we have our youth camps there each year. If you love the mountains, silence, and being away from the hustle and bustle of the city, you would love this place. We have been going there for about 35 years.

There, just off of a trail that we ride on, are some very tall pine trees. There are many of them. They stand straight. They stand tall. As you come up the trail, it looks like a congregation of saints standing tall praising and worshiping God. It is a beautiful sight. Then all at once you see a tree – just one tree. It is all bent over, even the top is touching the ground, and it hasn't grown like the rest of the trees.

This reminds me of when I was pastoring and I would look into the congregation, and the saints would be standing tall, hands raised worshiping God. All at once I would see somebody like this tree that is all bent out of shape. They are not standing, and they are not worshiping. Why are they bent out of shape? I don't know. I don't know what has happened in their past. I don't know what they have been through. All I know is the other trees are tall and straight, but this one is bent out of shape.

On this journey through life, we must be careful that we don't let something happen to us. When people think and speak of us, we do not want them to say that something happened to us, and we never got over it, and we are bent out of shape. So as we take inventory of our self, where are we at in our life? Are we in the congregation standing tall, praising and worshiping God? Or are we one, that when the pastor looks out over the congregation, he has a sinking feeling in his heart because we are bent out of shape, and he has never been able to get us where God wants us. Anyway, it is just a thought. Something to think about.

P.S. By the way, I just went back this summer to see that tree and the storms of the last winter blew it over. If we don't get over what has affected us and bent us out of shape in our spirit we will eventually lose out with God – think about it.

I've Been Down That Road Before

Now friend if you'll just listen to me
You'll get some good hard-earned advice
I don't aim to meddle in your business
I'm just tryin' to save you an awful price

Now you see these teeth that I ain't got
And these knots on my bald head
I'll guarantee you boys I didn't get them
There lyin' at home in the bed

Now take the smart aleck in any town
Of him folks want no part
He acts like his head was only
Made to hold his ears apart

Now he might not like what I'm bout to say
And my words might make him sore
But I'm just tryin' to be helpful cause
I've been down that road before

To bully folks and play mean tricks
Was once my pride and joy
Till one day I was toted home
And mama didn't know her little boy

My head was swelled up so big
I couldn't get it through my front door
Now I ain't just talkin' to hear myself cause
I've been down that road before
A little fellow about my size

Got tired of being pushed about
So he went to work and when he got through
He'd knocked every one of my teeth out
One time too many I'd rubbed him wrong

And he evened up the score
Now that's what happens when you
Get too big for your britches
I've been down that road before

Now when you get to thinkin' you're really smart
There's always somebody smarter than you
And no matter how much you boast and brag
You can still learn a thing or two

Go get you some treatments just like I've had
And you won't hanker for more
I really learned the meaning of living and loving
I've been down that road before

Now the man that walks this rocky road
Usually gets just what he deserves
Cause he's just a helpless servant to
A master that he serves

Now I've learned to slow my temper down
And not to pick no scraps no more
Boys it's a lot easier on the head and eyes
I've been down that road before

-Written by Douglas Williams, Leonard Williams,
 Melvin Williams
Good advice, huh!

Lesson 23
Just Deal with It

Remember, these lessons are to help us on the journey of life. Sometimes things happen like a jack-in-the-box; they just pop up. We have got to make a decision. Are we going to let it alone, ignore it, put it off, or try to forget it? But some things can't be ignored. They have to be dealt with. So we need to pray that God will give us the wisdom to know what to do with whatever has popped up in our life. Whatever it is, just deal with it.

The word "deal" means to take action with regard to someone or something, the act of dealing. Whatever it is, just deal with it. Sometimes we have to just back off and deal with it. "He that handleth a matter wisely shall find good." (Proverbs 16:20) So whatever we have to deal with, let us use wisdom. Get a handle on it and deal with it.

What's going on in our life right now that is bugging

us? Well, it could be that it is going to be there until we deal with it.

Well, I think I'll just quit writing right here, so you can go deal with it!

P.S. But remember to deal with it wisely. And remember, to deal with some things, you just leave them alone. If you've got to deal with it, go do it right now, if the time is right.

Lesson 24
Forbearing One Another

I therefore, the prisoner of the Lord, beseech you that ye walk worthy of the vocation wherewith ye are called, With all lowliness and meekness, with longsuffering, **forbearing one another in love**; (Ephesians 4:1-2)

Verse 2 tells us that we are to walk with lowliness, meekness, longsuffering, and **forbear** one another. On this journey called Life, there will be people, a lot of people. On the road of Life there will be some good and some bad. If we are to have peace and be successful, we have got to learn how to get along with others. Just to tell it like it is…some people will bug us. Some people are fun to be around and some are not, but we must learn to forebear. There may be someone reading this book right now saying, "Vaughn Morton really bugs me!" There could be some people that get on our nerves. We have got to learn to forebear. We must keep in mind that we may have something in our personality that bugs others.

Let us see what the Bible says about it. Verse 2 says we are to bear with one another in love and longsuffering. This is saying that we are to learn to put up with one another's faults. Make allowances for one another. Like the Bible says, " If it be possible, as much as lieth in you, live peaceably with all men." (Romans 12:18) To sum it all up...we have to learn to put up with one another, with all of our faults!

Lesson 25
Just Keep on Living for God

On the road of life things are going to happen, but no matter what happens just keep on living for God.

Finally, my brethren, be strong in the Lord, and in the power of his might. Put on the whole armour of God, that ye may be able to stand against the wiles of the devil. For we wrestle not against flesh and blood, but against principalities, against powers, against the rulers of the darkness of this world, against spiritual wickedness in high places. Wherefore take unto you the whole armour of God, that ye may be able to withstand in the evil day, and having done all, to stand. Stand therefore, having your loins girt about with truth, and having on the breastplate of righteousness; And your feet shod with the preparation of the gospel of peace; Above all, taking the shield of faith, wherewith ye shall be able to quench all the fiery darts of the wicked. And take the helmet of salvation, and the sword of the Spirit, which is the word of God: Praying always with all prayer and supplication in the Spirit, and watching thereunto with all perseverance and supplication for all saints; (Ephesians 6:10-18)

Note a portion of verse 13, "....in the evil day, and having done all, to stand." Verse 14 says, "stand therefore." In life the evil day will come. Trials will come. Temptations and tests will come. The Bible says, "having done all to stand, stand therefore." May I add these words, "Just keep on living for God."

Another way to say it, "Having done all to stand, stand therefore, and hold your ground." I Corinthians 15:58 teaches us, "....be ye steadfast, unmovable." To stand means to maintain one's position, to be firm and steadfast, to remain stationary, to maintain your ground as a victor. Having conquered all, stand ready to battle again, and just keep on living for God.

Don't Quit
When things go wrong as they sometimes will
When the road you're trudging seems all uphill
When the funds are low and the debts are high
And you want to smile, but you have to sigh
When care is pressing you down a bit
Rest if you must, but don't you quit
Life has its twists and turns
As every one of us sometimes learns
And many a fellow turns about
When he might have won, had he stuck it out
Don't give up though the pace seems slow
You may succeed with another blow

> Often the struggler has given up
> When he might have captured the victor's cup
> And he learned too late when the night came down
> How close he was to the golden crown
> And you never can tell how close you are
> It may be near when it seems afar
> So stick to the fight when you're hardest hit
> It's when things seem worst that you mustn't quit
> And just keep on living for God

Who shall separate us from the love of Christ? shall tribulation, or distress, or persecution, or famine, or nakedness, or peril, or sword? As it is written, For thy sake we are killed all the day long; we are accounted as sheep for the slaughter. Nay, in all these things we are more than conquerors through him that loved us. For I am persuaded, that neither death, nor life, nor angels, nor principalities, nor powers, nor things present, nor things to come, Nor height, nor depth, nor any other creature, shall be able to separate us from the love of God, which is in Christ Jesus our Lord. (Romans 8:35-39)

When we think about just keeping on living for God, we think about Bro. Job and ALL that he went through and ALL that he suffered, yet he never caved in. He never gave up, but in the midst of it all he just kept on living for God. What does the Bible say happened because he did not give up? It says, "So the LORD blessed the latter end of Job more than his beginning." (Job 42:12) If you want the blessing, you have to be steadfast, unmovable, and just keep on living for God. In the end the blessing will come and it will be worth it all.

Things will happen such as: they may not invite you to

the party, you may know someone that is a hypocrite, or you may be the only one living for God in your family, you may be the only one in your school that is an Apostolic Christian. Maybe you are going through a place where you can't feel God. Or could it be that sickness has come, or maybe you were rebuked by the pastor - that is an acid test. It could be that you didn't get the job in the church that you wanted, or what about that friend that let you down? The boss gave you a bad deal or could it be the loss of a loved one? Or maybe you have lost everything you have ever worked for. Or you have prayed and the answer hasn't come. Or you were the only one that showed up at the church on workday. Or you're getting older and still haven't found a husband or a wife. Or funds are low and debts are high. Or your girlfriend or boyfriend doesn't like you anymore. The list can go on and on and on, but the answer to all of this, whatever may come in life, is to make up your mind right now, <u>I am just going to keep on living for God</u>.

Lesson 26
Learning Our Lesson the First Time

"The difference between school and life?
In school, you're taught a lesson
And then given a test.
In life, you're given a test
That teaches you a lesson."
~Tom Bodett

We need to learn our lesson the first time.

There have been sometimes in life when I learned my lesson the first time. That is why I haven't done it the second time..... Go learn what that means!

Lesson 27
Learn What to Pay Attention To

Oh yes, as we make our way through life, we can't or must not stop to chase every dog that comes out to bark at us. If we do, we will just end up in life known as the person that chases dogs.

When you are hunting for deer you don't go chasing rabbits or shooting at every rabbit that jumps up. In other words, in life we can't chase every rumor that we hear. We can't be offended at everything that is said about us. Maybe we could just say, "Don't be so sensitive." The lesson here is to learn what to pay attention to in life. Chasing dogs and rabbits can get us off course. So, learn what to pay attention to.

Lesson 28
True Blue

Many years ago, I was preaching for Elder I. H. Terry in Bakersfield, and I made a comment about a young couple in his church.

I said, "Bro. Terry, that seems to be a fine young couple."

He said, "I don't know, so far so good. If I was preaching their funeral today, I could say good things. Bro. Morton, they haven't finished yet. You don't judge a thing before its time." He continued, "Time and circumstances will reveal what we are. In life a person will come sometime, somewhere, someday, somehow to what he really is."

So it is in life. We see someone who is making great strides, and all at once they are shipwrecked. They finally came to what they really are. Let us make sure that on this journey we stay true to God, to others and to ourselves. Let us prove to all that we really are as the old saying goes "true blue."

Lesson 29
Life

Life can be like the six year old boy that quit school. One morning he went to get on the bus but didn't. Instead, he went back home.

His mother said, "Jason, why are you back home?"

He said, "Momma, I decided to quit school today."

She said, "Why?"

He said, "<u>It's too long, it's too hard and it's too boring.</u>"

His mother said, "Jason, you have just described life. Sometimes it seems too long, too hard, and too boring. That is what we call life. Now go get on the bus."

When we feel like life is too long, too hard and too boring, we still must go get on the bus. Just keep on keeping on. A better day will come.

Lesson 30
Life Can Be a Circus

But if we hope for that we see not, then do we with patience wait for it. (Romans 8:25)

Life is like a kid trying to watch a circus parade through a knothole in a fence. When you look through a knothole you can only see what is right in front of you. Sometimes we get something fixed in our mind that we really want to see. Maybe it is the lions. If we are not careful we will not enjoy the other acts, like the clowns and the monkeys, because we are so impatient to see the lions. We have to remember that everything is arranged in a certain order for a purpose. Some things can't go right next to each other, like lions and monkeys, because one would attack the other. Some acts are to get us ready for something else. We need to have faith that the lions are there in our parade. They are coming, but we just can't see them yet. Whatever it is that we really want and dream for in life, it will come in its time. But remember, we must pray, "God, Your will, Your way, Your time." In the meantime, let's enjoy whatever is in front of us today. Don't be so full of anxiety, worry and stress that we don't enjoy what is passing by us right now. Remember that each day is a day that the Lord hath made, let us rejoice and be glad in it.

Cast not away therefore your confidence, which hath great recompence of reward. For ye have need of patience, that, after ye have done the will of God, ye might receive the promise. (Hebrews 10:35-36)

Lesson 31
Life Takes Time

One day, I was talking to my youngest grandson, Judson. When he was just a little thing, his sister Adriel started calling him Juddy Buddy. So one day, I was with Juddy Buddy. I don't remember what the conversation was, but I just said to him, "You know, Juddy, life takes time." I didn't think any more about it. Later, at another time, we were in an In-N-Out restaurant. We tried to beat the crowd, but all at once there was a long line. I said, "Juddy, look at that line. I am glad we are not in that line." He said, "But, Papa, remember, life takes time."

That got to working on me, and I thought, "You know, life really does take time." Let's talk about it a little bit, a little seed thought, and you can take it from there.

We want to hurry up and get there so we can hurry up and get back. Sometimes in getting there and getting back, the unexpected happens, and we are reminded that life takes time. Jesus said, "In your patience possess ye your souls." (Luke 21:19) Elder Paul Price said, "If we are going to be saved, we have got to have patience."

Cast not away therefore your confidence, which hath great recompence of reward. For ye have need of patience, that, after ye have done the will of God, ye might receive the promise. (Hebrews 10:35, 36)

These scriptures tell us that life takes time. The Bible teaches us, "...and let us run with patience the race that is set before us." (Hebrews 12:1) Bro. James tells us, "let patience have her perfect work." (James 1:4) In other words, life takes time. I am reminded of when I was a teenager and had transferred to a new school I had never been to before. Some other boys and I were new at this school. They told us to go down to the boy's gym and sit on the bench outside of the door. In a few moments, a P.E. teacher walked out. His name was Mr. McGuire. He said, "Boys, sit right here and let me tell you something. Remember in life there will be a lot of waiting." He was telling us that life takes time. The Bible has a lot to say about patience, longsuffering, and waiting.

Here is a young couple, and they are expecting their first child, but remember life takes time. It will be nine more months. Think about it, at the store we wait in line. At the red light, we wait again. At the dentist office, we wait. At the stop sign, there we are again. We come to a school zone and it says SLOW. What it is really saying is life takes time. We are going down the highway and want to go 75 mph, but the sign says 55 mph.

Let's slow down and realize that life takes time. Stop and smell the roses.

P.S. The next time someone asks, "Where have you been? Why didn't you hurry up?" Tell them, "Remember Elder Morton says, 'Life takes time.'"

Lesson 32
The Unexpected Cross

Boast not thyself of to morrow; for thou knowest not what a day may bring forth. (Proverbs 27:1)

Whereas ye know not what shall be on the morrow. (tomorrow) (James 4:14)

And as they led him (Jesus) away, they laid hold upon one Simon, a Cyrenian, coming out of the country, and on him they laid the cross, that he might bear it after Jesus. (Luke 23:26)

As you just read in the book of Proverbs, "Thou knowest not what a day may bring forth." Then in the book of James, we "know not what shall be on the morrow." We do not know what a day may bring forth.

Then we find in Luke 23:26, a man named Simon came that day to see (watch) the crucifixion of Jesus. He no doubt, when he got up that morning, had no idea that he would have to carry the cross that Jesus was crucified on. So we would call this, for that day, the <u>unexpected cross</u>.

Simon of Cyrene did not know that an unexpected cross was waiting for him that day. No doubt he said to himself, and maybe even to others, as we sometimes say in life, "I just wasn't expecting this."

"Then said Jesus unto his disciples, If any man will come after me, let him deny himself, and take up his cross, and follow me." (Mathew 16:24) If you notice in Luke 9:23 it says, "take up his cross daily." "And he that taketh not his cross, and followeth after me, is not worthy of me." (Mathew 10:38)

Unexpected means not expected, unforeseen, surprising or unanticipated.

As we take this journey through life, we just don't know what cross we might have to bear before life is over. Someone said, "He that has no cross, will have no crown." Benjamin Franklin said, "After crosses and losses, men grow humbler and wiser."

Hebrews 12:2 says, "... for the joy that was set before him endured the cross." The joy that was set before Jesus was, if He endured the cross, He would purchase His blood-washed church. If we endure the unexpected crosses that may be laid upon our shoulders, there will be a reward. Sometimes we just have to endure our cross. The Bible says he that endureth until the end the same shall be saved. It will be worth it all when we see Jesus.

Just a few examples. Maybe it is a sickness that falls upon a spouse and the other has to take care of them for years. Maybe it is the loss of a loved one, or something that is out of our control, yet it brings much difficulty to our home. I am sure you know of situations where it was an unexpected cross. One thing I do know we must learn to bear our cross with dignity.

Tears
They say that life is a highway
and its mile-stones are the years,
And now and then there is a toll-gate
where you buy your way with tears.
It's a rough road and steep road,
and it stretches broad and far,
But at last it leads to a golden town
where golden houses are.

Boast not thyself of to morrow; for thou knowest not what a day may bring forth. (Proverbs 27:1)

Don't fear the future.
Don't fear the unexpected.
For God is already there.

Lesson 33
A Helpless Feeling

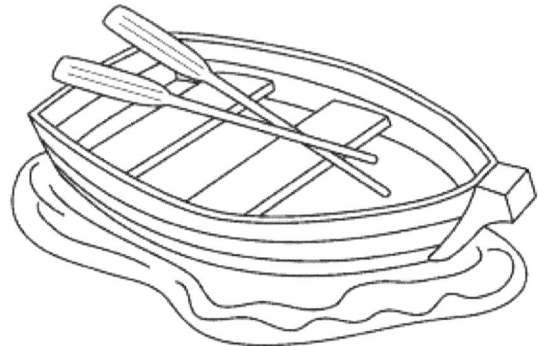

Several years ago, I flew to Phoenix, Arizona. I was picked up by a man in a van to take me to a hotel. As we were driving along he said he was in the San Diego fire of 2003. He said, "I felt so helpless. The fire was all around me, and the only place I could go was in the ocean, but I didn't have a boat."

We will come to a place in life where we will feel helpless, and we won't have a boat.

At a moment like that we need to trust God's Word, when it says in "For he hath said, I will never leave thee, nor forsake thee. So that we may boldly say, The Lord is my helper, and I will not fear what man shall do unto me." (Hebrews 13:5, 6)

So in those seemingly helpless moments, remember God is Always There!

There hath no temptation taken you but such as is common to man: but God is faithful, who will not suffer you to be tempted above that ye are able; but will with the temptation also make a way to escape, that ye may be able to bear it. (1 Corinthians 10:13)

P.S. The man did escape – he was there to tell the story. When we trust God there will always be a way of escape.

Lesson 34
Loneliness

*I watch, and am as a sparrow alone
upon the house top.* (Psalms 102:7)

The word that stands out to me in this scripture is the word alone. On this journey of life, there can be some lonely moments. The dictionary states that loneliness causes a depressing feeling of being alone or lonesome. All people, married or unmarried, young or old, at times feel the spirit of loneliness.

Perhaps there is no person that has ever graced this earth who was lonelier than Jesus Christ. He said, "Behold, the hour cometh, yea, is now come, that ye shall be scattered, every man to his own, and shall leave me **alone**..." (John 16:32)

In Isaiah 53:3 there is a prophecy concerning Jesus,

"He is despised and rejected of men; a man of sorrows, and acquainted with grief." Remember, Jesus went to the Garden of Gethsemane. Which reminds me of this little poem...

> Down shadowy lanes, across strange streams,
> Bridged over by our broken dreams;
> Behind the misty caps of years,
> Beyond the great salt fount of tears,
> The garden lies; strive as you may,
>
> You cannot miss it on your way.
> All paths that have been, or shall be,
> Pass somewhere through Gethsemane.
>
> All those who journey, soon or late,
> Must pass within the garden's gate;
> Must kneel alone in darkness there,
> And battle with some fierce despair.
>
> ~ "Gethsemane"
> by Ella Wheeler Wilcox

The Apostle Paul knew what it meant to dwell in loneliness. He said, "At my first answer no man stood with me, but all men forsook me." (II Timothy 4:16)

Loneliness can be caused by many things: a breakdown in communications, a breakdown in relationships, a crisis such as death or divorce, etc. I am sure that we have all experienced things like the little saying says:

Tears that fall on the outside, quickly vanish away,
But tears that fall on the inside, they stay and stay.

It could be that you are reading this book and smiling on the outside but crying on the inside.

Loneliness creates its casualties.

Black Friday was the first full day after the crash of the New York Stock Exchange. At the close of this very shocking day, two very successful businessmen who were good friends, visited long into the night. They explored together various possibilities of recuperation. Every door seemed to be closed. Finally, both of them went home to their families. Both of them were the same age. They had equal talent and possibilities. The next morning, both of them rose at approximately the same time. The difference in the two was that one of them went to his office and jumped out the window. The other reasoned that he still had his health, his family, and his God. Other than the fact that he was minus his money, he was essentially the same man he had been one month before. He believed that he could build back his empire, and he did. The other man felt like he stood alone and that there was absolutely no recourse for him. One had sufficient inward strength to survive. The other was utterly crushed.

Loneliness causes us to face the truth about ourselves. Like the old saying, "It is the truth that hurts." Many times loneliness reveals in us what we need to deal with. It is in loneliness that a person becomes fully acquainted with himself. It is there that we are prepared to come to grips with tragedy.

However painful it might be, it is needful, and we cannot grow without it.

If we are to survive some of the disappointments of

life, there must come to us a time of lonely reflection. If it does not come then, we become like an old serpent who cannot shed his skin.

Loneliness can come like a human presence whose power is silent, invisible, and indescribable. It is in loneliness that a greater spiritual life can be born within us. It is in loneliness that God develops us for His service. Though loneliness is a painful frightening thing, it is an ingredient of life which cannot be left out. Thus, our attitude should be that the experience of loneliness in our life is a constructive experience. We should always allow God to use it for our good. "Jacob was left alone..." (Genesis 32:24) In reading the history of Jacob's life we find that much of it was spent in grief, loneliness, and pain. All of these ingredients were necessary to prepare him for the major role of "Israel".

> "Our crosses are hewn from different trees,
> But we must all have our Calvaries;
> We may climb the height from a different side,
> But we each go up to be crucified.
> As we scale the steep, another may share
> The dreadful load that our shoulders bear;
> But the costliest sorrow is all our own,
> For on the summit we bleed alone."
> ~ Author Unkown

Someone once said, "I think I am in this world to find beauty in lonely places."

I have experienced camping by myself. I have been far back in the woods alone. I could feel the loneliness, but when I stopped and looked around, I could see the beauty of the woods in that lonely place. When we are in a lonely place, like in a deep valley, we need to look around and discover that Jesus is the Lily of the Valley. Like the song says:

> Long and winding road
> Keep on leading me
> Up ahead, I see a sign
> That points me straight ahead to victory
> I know I must be traveling right
> For I remember passing Calvary
> Although it's dusty and it's old
> For years its bore the traveler's load
> Someday this road will turn to gold.
> ~ "Long Winding Road" by Mickie Mangun

"So David and his men came to the city, and behold, it was burned with fire; and their wives, and their sons, and their daughters, were taken captives. Then David and the people that were with him lifted up their voice and wept, until they had no more power to weep." (I Samuel 30:3-4) Their sons, daughters, and wives had been taken away. Don't you know that a spirit of loneliness filled their hearts? "And David was greatly distressed; for the people spake of stoning him, because the soul of all the people was grieved, every man for his sons and for his daughters: but David encouraged himself in the LORD his God." (Verse 6) Note that it says <u>David encouraged himself in the Lord</u>. When we are in a lonely place, we must learn to encourage ourselves in the Lord. When David did, God gave him a word to pursue the enemy. In verse 18, David recovered all that the Amalekites had carried away. When in a lonely places, if we will truly turn to God, He will give us the answer. There will be a better day. Have faith in God. Everything is going to be alright

... for he hath said, I will never leave thee, nor forsake thee. (Hebrews 13:5)

....lo, I am with you alway, even unto the end of the world. (Mathew 28:20)

A man that hath friends must shew himself friendly: and there is a friend that sticketh closer than a brother. (Proverbs 18:24)

> "They say that life is a highway
>   and its milestones are years,
> And now and then there's a toll-gate
>   where you buy your way with tears.
> It's a rough road and a steep road
>   and it stretches broad and far,
> But at last it leads to a golden Town
>   where golden Houses are."
>   ~ "Roofs" by Joyce Kilmer

I say.... "And we are never alone again."

Lesson 35
Lonely Times

God left him, to try him, that he might know all that was in his heart. (2 Chronicles 32:31)

Like David said, "My God, my God, why hast thou forsaken me? why art thou so far from helping me, and from the words of my roaring? O my God, I cry in the daytime, but thou hearest not; and in the night season, and am not silent." (Psalms 22:1-2)

There can be lonely stretches in life and we say, "Where is God?" It is like one service I was preaching when Tyler Gregg was about four years old. He was sitting with Juanita Barnes. In my preaching I said very loudly with emphasis, "God is in this place!" Little Tyler looked all around and said to Juanita, "Where is God?" Juanita said to him, "He is everywhere." Tyler said, "He is hiding, huh?!"

Sometimes it seems that God is hiding as it was in the days in Hezekiah when the Bible said God left him to try him that He might know all that was in his heart. Many years ago an elder preacher friend was pastoring and going through a hard time. God was silent. He told his wife, "I am going into that bedroom and I am not coming out till I get an answer." After a while he came out and his wife said to him, "What did he say?" The elder said, "He ain't talking."

If you have lived for God any length of time, you have gone through a time where it seems that God is hiding. He is silent. He is not talking. I remember one time that I was going through a time such as this. I remember going to the church and praying and praying. I was so desperate that I looked up and said with a loud voice, "God, God, I am over here!" It felt like God didn't know where I was. As the scripture says, "But they that wait upon the LORD shall renew their strength; they shall mount up with wings as eagles; they shall run, and not be weary; and they shall walk, and not faint." (Isaiah 40:31)

At a time like this we must be patient and wait on God. We must not act on our own. He will break His silence. We are His children, and He loves us.

Lesson 36
Dealing with Losses

"A time to get, and a time to lose;"
– Ecclesiastes 3:6

This scripture tells us that somewhere and sometime in life we will deal with a loss. In other words, we have got to deal with losing. Something we have or something with us is going away. We must learn to cope or deal with losses.

Definition of losses: An instance of losing, to suffer loss through death, final separation, no longer visible, taken away, beyond reach.

I was not born or raised in Pentecost. I came into the church just before I turned 16. I had a wonderful pastor I loved very much. He put good things in me. I will forever be thankful for him, his wisdom, and all that he taught me. He and I were very close. After being in the church for several years, with his blessing, I went evangelizing, but I always stayed in touch with him.

> *It is very important for us to have an elder in our life.*

Twenty years after I came into the church, my pastor, Bro. J. E. Rode, passed away. I had evangelized for several years, pastored for three years, evangelized again and then was pastoring again here in Fresno. To me, it was a great loss that I had to cope with. You probably did not know him; to you it is just a story. To this day, at least once or twice a year, I go to his grave to thank God for this good man God had placed in my life. We that knew him and loved him did not think we could live without him. But many, many years have passed and we have learned to live with the loss.

So prepare yourself, for in life there will be losses. We have to learn to live without. If we know someone that has a loss, I am reminded of the following story... sometimes we do not have words to say but we can cry with them.

A little girl lost a playmate in death and one day she reported to her family that she had gone to comfort the sorrowing mother. "What did you say to her," asked the father. "Nothing," the little girl replied, "I just climbed up on her lap and cried with her."

Tears that fall on the outside, quickly vanish away, but tears that fall on the inside, they stay, and they stay and they stay. Some people are smiling but on the inside they are crying.

Lesson 37
Change

On this journey of life we have to expect change. Tomorrow everything will change. I have lived long enough to see that life is full of changes. The dictionary says change is an act or a process. It means to give a different position or direction, to make or become different, to pass from one phase to another.

Yes, tomorrow everything can change. Change will come.

Life is full of adjustments.

One phase of life ends and another begins. Sometimes change is so gradual that we do not notice life's changing scenes. Time and change waits for no one. It is like the eye doctor says, "One day you realize that you are in a phase of life when it is normal to need bifocals. It crept upon us unaware."

Time and change happens to us all. Do we learn from them? Or do we try to hold on to the past? Do we resist change, or can we flow with change? If we resist change then we will live out our lives being miserable and blaming God.

This is the way that God has planned it. He planned the changing seasons of nature; He also planned the changing seasons of life. Yes, tomorrow everything can change.

God commands or allows the winds and storms of life. Everything in life is in His control. Jesus said, "What I do thou knowest not now." (John 13:7) Some things that we do not understand are the foundation or the springboard for what God has planned for our life.

King Solomon said, "To every thing there is a season and a time to every purpose under the heaven." (Ecclesiastes 3:1)

Yes, tomorrow everything can change. We grow from childhood through teen-hood, into adulthood and finally we reach old-hood. Through the years we witness many changes.

People get married, move to new neighborhoods, change jobs, have children. Our children grow up and leave the home. Our parents grow old. Everything changes in time.

We must not expect things to stay the same. Some changes we witness are good, and we are glad for the change; we say this is good. Other times, the change is not good.

Sometimes we question change. We must remember that all things work together for good to them that love God. Some changes can reveal what we really are....go learn what that means.

We must remember that God never changes. God said, "I am the Lord, I change not." (Malachi 3:6) It is good to remember what Brother Paul said, "I have learned, in whatsoever state I am, therewith to be content." (Philippians 4:11)

Ecclesiastes 3:11 says, "He hath made every thing beautiful in his time."

In the process of time, we may understand why some changes have come to our life. Then again, we may never understand. That is when we need to remember Proverbs 3:5, "Trust in the LORD with all thine heart; and lean not unto thine own understanding." And remember, change will come. Are you ready?

Lesson 38
Seasons

To every thing there is a season, and a time to every purpose under the heaven: (Ecclesiastes 3:1)

God made the seasons.

And God said, Let there be lights in the firmament of the heaven to divide the day from the night; and let them be for signs, and for seasons, and for days, and years: (Genesis 1:14)

Seedtime and harvest, and cold and heat, summer and winter, and day and night. (Genesis 8:22)

Life has seasons and if we don't understand that we can get frustrated.

Leviticus 26:4 *I will give you rain in due season*

Numbers 9:3 *His appointed season*
II Chronicles 15:3 *A long season*
Job 5:26 *A shuck of corn cometh in his season*
Job 30:17 *The night season*
Psalms 1:3 *Bringeth forth his fruit in his season*
Daniel 7:12 *Prolonged for a season*
Luke 4:13 *He departeth for a season*
John 5:4 *Certain season*
John 5:35 *A season to rejoice*
Acts 13:11 *Not seeing the sun for a season*
Acts 24:25 *A convenient season*
II Timothy 4:2 *Be instant in season and out of season*
Revelations 6:11 *A little season*
Daniel 2:21 *He changeth the time and the seasons*
Acts 20:18 *Paul said I have been with you in ALL seasons.*

The word season means a period of time. A season can be long or short. We can enjoy some seasons, and some we don't. We are not in charge of the seasons.....God is!

Remember, Abraham forced the season by having a child with Hagar. He did not wait on God. Seasons have purpose, and they have reason. Don't try to run away from the season. We must stay faithful in our season.

To every thing there is a season, and a time to every purpose under the heaven: (Ecclesiastes 3:1)

He hath made every thing beautiful in his time [or season!] (Ecclesiastes 3:11)

What season of life are we in right now?

And let us not be weary in well doing: for in due season we shall reap, if we faint not. (Galatians 6:9)

Lesson 39
Old Age

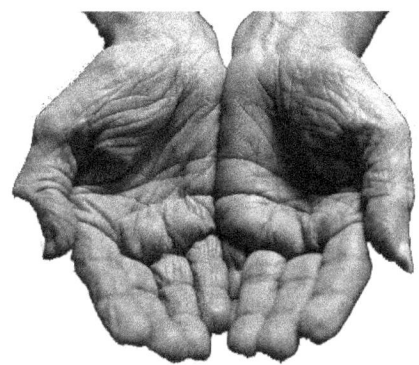

As we make this journey through life, we come to a place that we call "Old Age." Now before I get into this lesson, let me say you may not enjoy it. You may just want to skip it. What I am going to talk about will happen to each of us if the Lord tarries. So may I say, "Remember, LIFE happens, and we must be prepared for it."

You know the Bible does say in the book of Ecclesiastes, "A time to be born and a time to die." It is like David said, "I have been young, and now am old." (Psalms 37:25) I can say that about myself. I was young. There was a time when I was just a boy and then a teenager, but life kept happening. Now I am 77 years old (2017).

The book of Ecclesiastes, chapter 12, talks about old age. Verse one says, "Remember now thy Creator in the days of thy youth, while the evil days come not, nor the years draw nigh, when though shalt say, I have no pleasure in them." That scripture is talking about old age. You can go ahead and read verses one through seven for yourself. Verse seven says, "Then shall the dust return to the earth as it was and the spirit shall return unto God who gave it." It is like Elder I. H. Terry said, "Sun rise and sun set. Sun rise and sun set. Sun rise and sun set. Then you wake up and you are old."

Come to think of it, I don't think I like this lesson myself. But I believe in facing reality. By the grace of God, I want to grow old with dignity. The Bible does have a lot to say about age and gray hair. Such as when the Lord said unto Abram, "thou shall be buried in a good old age." (Genesis 15:15) "Now Abraham and Sarah were old and well stricken in age." (Genesis 18:11) You husbands and wives get ready to grow old together.

Joshua of old realized that growing old was part of life. He didn't try to hide from it. He didn't try to shun it or deny it. "And Joshua called for all Israel, and for their elders, and for their heads, and for their judges, and for their officers, and said unto them, I am old and stricken in age." (Joshua 23:2) He realized that life's evening sun was sinking low. A few more days and he must go. So he began to set things in order.

Even the great Apostle Paul grew old. The book of Philemon says, "Paul the aged..." (Philemon verse 9) There are some things that go with old age that we don't like. Such as Genesis 48:10 says, "Now the eyes of Israel were dimmed for age, so that he could not see." II Chronicles 36:17 talks about being "stooped for age." It can happen.

Gray hair, according to the Bible, goes with age. The

Bible says, "The beauty of old men is the gray head (women too)." (Proverbs 20:29) "The hoary (gray) head is a crown of glory." (Proverbs 16:31) Let me just drop this in, in passing. God is not pleased if we dye our hair, regardless if you are a man or a woman, when He has allowed it to turn gray. The Bible says, "It is a crown of glory." "With us are both the grayheaded and the very aged men (women)." (Job 15:10)

So we have established the fact that we do grow old. In my lifetime I have watched a lot of people grow old. Such as, my dad and mother, my pastor Bro. J.E. Rode, my grandmothers, my grandfather, my uncles and my aunts, loved ones, and friends. My dad and mother were good American people. The kind of people that the real America was made of. We were just poor folks from West Texas – farmers raising cotton, maize, hogs, cows, horses, etc. After World War II we came to California. At the time I was just a young boy and did not know that God was leading me to this Acts 2:38 Pentecostal truth. I have watched my daddy and mamma grow old. My mother died at age 78. My dad lived another 12 years. He could take care of himself, and he never remarried. My sister, Brenda, and her husband Stan, watched after him. Their help was a blessing to me and I am forever thankful. My dad got older, and there came a day that he had to sell his house and move into assisted living. The doctor said he couldn't drive anymore. He no longer had a dog and he always had a dog. He lived to be 93 years old. One day, I was talking to him and he said, "I once had a wife. I once had my home and my car and my dog, and now I have nothing." This is what you call life. It happens.

David said, "Cast me not off in the time of old age,

forsake me not when my strength faileth." (Psalms 71:9) The Lord says, "Even to your old age I am he; and even to your hoar (gray) hairs will I carry you." (Isaiah 46:4) If we live for God and do our best, God is going to take care of us.

We, as old people, have a place in the kingdom of God. "Those that be planted in the house of the LORD shall flourish in the courts of our God. They shall still bring forth fruit in old age." (Psalms 92:13-14) We may not be as strong in our old age, but we can bear fruit in our old age. We can share our wisdom. We can pray, etc.

My prayer is, "God help me to grow old with dignity and bring forth fruit in old age." I want to be the kind of old person that younger men and women and young people would want to be around. As long as God leaves us here, we must have something to offer.

Lesson 40
It Will Never Be Like It Was

"This one thing I do, forgetting those things which are behind, and reaching forth unto those things which are before." (Philippians 3:13)

Elder Paul Price and I were riding in my car in Fresno, California, in September of 2008. He was 86 and I was 68. We were talking about some of the bygone days and how good it was. Bro. Price said to me, "<u>It will never be like it was</u>." Sometimes in life we try to hold on to the moment, to the hour, to the day. We never want to let it go. We want to keep it this way forever, but change comes, and we must face the reality of life. Things never stay the same. Sometimes we must come to the place that it will never be like it was, and we have to adjust. We cannot hold on to some things; they will go. Sometimes we try to recreate what used to be, but we can't. So we must just get over it and move on. All moments and hours and days are not equal.

Then there are times in life that we never want it to be like it was. I am only putting this on the table, you are going to have to sort it out for yourself.

Lesson 41
Sorting It All Out

Sometimes on this journey called Life, we have got to sit down and sort it all out. Some people sit and think. Other people just sit. To get through life, sometimes we have got to sit and think and sort it out. Proverbs 20:5, "Counsel in the heart of man is like deep water; but a man of understanding will draw it out." Sometimes our thoughts are like deep water. We have to think very deep. I was talking to a friend, and I could feel that something was on their mind. Very deep in their heart and thoughts. I said to them, "What are you thinking? Or what is on your mind?" They said, "Nothing..." I said "Oh yes, there is." They said, "Well, I am just trying to sort it all out."

Sorting means to arrange, to put in a certain place, sorting bad apples from the good, to put in order, to go over mentally.

A preacher friend of mine, when he sits down to eat, arranges all of his food just right. If he is eating M&Ms he will put all the same color in a certain place. He is interesting to watch.

Like a puzzle, we look for the pieces to bring it all together. Sometimes we just have to sit and think. One day I was cleaning my garage and was sorting things out. I had five boxes. Box one was stuff to throw away. Box two goes to the church. Box three goes in the house. Box four goes in the car. Box five goes in the garage.

That is the way life is sometimes, we have to sort it out. We wait. We think. We pray. We read. We talk. We search. We feel after. We listen. We worship. We are sorting it out. We are trying to find our way.

Well, that is all of that. Now go sit and think and sort it out.

Lesson 42
One Day at a Time, Brother, One Day at a Time

When Elder I. H. Terry was alive and with us, he taught me a good lesson. I called him one day and said, "Elder, give me a word from God." He immediately answered, "One day at a time, brother, one day at a time." I know that is just a simple thought, but it will bring peace to our hearts if we will pay attention to it and really realize the past is gone; it's behind us. The future is out of our reach. We can only live one day at time. So let's just relax, and do the best we can today. Tomorrow will take care of itself.

For remember Jesus said, "Therefore I say unto you, Take no thought for your life." (Matthew 6:25) In other words, to put it in simple terms, He was saying don't worry. He says, "Take therefore no thought for the morrow." (Matthew 6:34)

The Apostle Paul gave some good advice, "Be careful for nothing," (Philippians 4:6) which means don't worry. He went on to say, "....but in every thing by prayer and supplication with thanksgiving let your request be made known unto God." Then he said, "And the peace of God, which passeth all understanding, shall keep your hearts and minds through Christ Jesus." (verse 7) In other words, like the Elder said, "One day at a time, brother, one day at a time." To tell you the truth I have learned I am no superman. I can only take it one day at a time. So, relax. Oh, by the way, that reminds me of something else I learned. We will call it "Life" and it went something like this....

> Life can be sweet if we approach it right. I like what one woman said, "A nice cup of tea is like liquid sunshine. Carefully fill your teakettle with cold water and bring it to a true boil, then let the tea leaves steep for exactly five long minutes. So the flavor will blossom." You know there are some things in life that shouldn't be hurried. I have learned that brewing a proper pot of tea is a lot like living a proper life. It takes extra effort, but it is always worth it.

So live life one day at a time. Make a masterpiece out of it. Just let it unfold.

Lesson 43
The Stress of Life and Balance

As I take this journey called Life, there is one thing that is unavoidable. We have got to deal with it. It is called stress. Jesus said, "And take heed to yourselves, lest at any time your hearts be overcharged with surfeiting, and drunkenness, <u>and the cares of this life</u>. . ." (Luke 21:34)

The cares of life.... just everyday life and things that we have to deal with. Such as the job, the washing machine, the refrigerator that stopped working, the car that broke down, raising children, paying bills, the leak in the roof and the list goes on. You can make your own list because you know what life is. You know what may be really stressing you right now.

Strong's Exhaustive Concordance of the Bible translates the "cares of life" as written in Luke 21:34 as "the distractions of life." We are all aware that we are living in the last days and the pressure is on. You may feel all alone in the struggle of life and stress, but you are not. This is common to man. Daniel 7:25 talks about the saints of the most High wearing out. Revelation 12:12 talks about the devil knowing that he has but a short time. The pressure is on. Stress and burnout is real.

I took this from Richard Exley's book called the *Rhythm of Life*. It is not in print anymore, but if you can find a copy, buy it. He said this:

I'm tired, Lord.
Bone weary from the inside out.
I'm tired of a constantly cluttered desk
And an overcrowded calendar.
I'm tired of broken things.
I'm tired of problems I can't solve,
And hurts I can't heal.
I'm tired of deadlines and decisions
Duties done without any pleasure.
I'm tired, Lord.
I really am.
My creative juices are at a low ebb.
I have no inspiration,
No insight,
No freshness.
It's been some time now
Since I felt truly alive.
I can't remember
The last time I walked barefoot in the park,
Or lay on my back in the grass watching the clouds,
I'm homesick for the mountains,
For the smell of pines after a rain,
For the sound of the wind in the aspens.
I'm hungry for home-baked bread and country cream,

Home-canned peaches,
And fresh tomatoes right off the vine.
I want to feel.
I want to laugh and cry.
I want to live life to the fullest.
I want to love, and be loved.
Forgive me, Lord.
Sometimes I get so caught up in my work,
And that which comes on me daily
That I miss life's best
I'm tired, Lord. Please help me.

Yes, stress and burn out are really real. The Apostle Paul was not a superman. He was a human being just like you and I, and he said in II Corinthians 1:8, "For we would not, brethren, have you ignorant of our trouble which came to us in Asia, that we were <u>pressed out of measure</u>, above strength, insomuch that we despaired even of life."

Note what he said, pressed out of measure, above strength. This can happen to us all.

- Nerves can be rubbed raw.
- We can be frustrated.
- If we are not careful, we can have an anger outburst.
- We can become resentful.
- Bills to be paid, debts are high, the funds are low.
- And because of all of this, our attitude can be bad. We can take on the spirit that life is not fair.

Elder I. H. Terry told me, "If we get mad at everything we want to get mad at, we will stay mad all the time." So that is not the solution. We can be overextended, overworked, have a crowded calendar. We can come to a place where all the joy is taken out of life. We can be tired inside and out. Life can be flat and tasteless. We can't quite get a handle on life. We can't seem to get it all together. The goodness of life has escaped us. Do we control life, or does life control us? Jesus was talking about the last days and said, "Except those days be shortened, there should no flesh be saved." (Matthew 24:22) Hey! But we are on this journey. We are trying to reach heaven and this is part of the journey.

The pressure is on. Do you ever feel like you are on a railroad track and the train is coming behind you? You are running as fast as you can down the track. The pressure is on! Life can be go, go, go, push, push, push. Stress is intensity. The definition of intensity is a physical, chemical or emotional factor that causes bodily or mental tension.

Stress can make the heart beat faster, and the lungs breath deeper. Tremendous energy can be released, which tenses the muscles so that we are ready to react. Prolonged stress tires the body, burns out the emotions and dulls the spirit. Jesus understands our stress. He was God in the flesh, and He was tempted in all points as we are.

Peter said, "Master, the multitude throng thee and press thee." (Luke 8:45) Jesus felt the pressures of life. "And he [Jesus] said unto them [the apostles], Come ye yourselves apart into a desert place, and rest a while: for there were many coming and going, and they had no leisure so much as to eat." (Mark 6:31) That's bad!

Jesus said to Peter, "Launch out into the deep, and let down your nets for a draught. And Simon answering said unto him, Master, we have toiled all night, and have taken nothing." (Luke 5:4-5) Sometimes we have toiled and worked so hard and see such little results, but we need to keep in mind what the Apostle Paul said, "And let us not be weary in well doing: for in due season we shall reap, if we faint not." (Galatians 6:9)

The word "toiled" means to feel fatigued, to work hard, to become weary, reducing in strength. In the dictionary toiled is defined as hard and continuous work and exhausting labor or effort.

Bro. Elijah, in I Kings 19:4, says that he sat down under a juniper tree, and he requested for himself that he might die. He said, "It is enough; now, O LORD, take away my life."

Remember, Bro. Paul said, "That which cometh upon me daily." (II Corinthians 11:28) How much of this stress do we bring on ourselves, and how much stress do we put on others? Working is right, and some people pride themselves in being a work-a-holic. We must learn to come aside and rest awhile.

We need balance in our life. I dealt with a person one time, concerning balance; they had an attitude. They looked me in the face and said, "Balance, balance, balance... I am sick of hearing that!" I do not rejoice in this, but that person lost out with God. Balance is important in every phase of our life.

I mentioned earlier the book *The Rhythm of Life*, in which the author deals with balance. He writes about four areas of life. I have rearranged it some for I feel it fits this situation better.

Number one, we need worship. That includes, prayer, Bible reading, and church-going. In other words spiritual things need to be number one.

Number two, we need work. One of the first things in

the Garden of Eden was to assign man the responsibility to tend the garden.

Number three, we need rest. Even Jesus and His disciples had to go aside for some rest.

Last but not least, we need some play in our life. Every once in a while I say to myself, "Self, this is play day." Then I just do something real enjoyable. Sometimes, when I get all my grandkids together, I do not condemn myself, I just say, "This is play time." For instance, ever so often, I will get Mark, Farah, Adriel, Cline, Judson, Nathan, KC, Drew, Gentry and Alayna together and we go to Disneyworld or Disneyland and just play.

Let's practice the rhythm of life.

Worship, Work, Rest and Play.

Now this is just a seed thought, you will have to work it out for yourself. Do something before you crack up under stress. Remember it is Worship, Work, Rest and Play.

Lesson 44
Money Answereth All Things

On this road called Life, we have what we call money. It takes money to make this journey. The Bible says, "Money answereth all things." (Ecclesiastes 10:19) Some would interpret that, "If I had enough money, I could do anything and everything I want." This is true, to a certain extent, but I think there is a deeper meaning here. Money tells me some things about myself. Money tells me some things about others. With money comes responsibility. A man's treatment of money is the most decisive test of his character. How he makes it and how he spends it. Yes, money tells us a lot about our self and others. It is a test of our true character.

The way a person pays their bills or doesn't pay them; if a person owes something and is not paying. What about their taxes? Even Jesus paid taxes. Where are we with the IRS? What about our tithes and offerings? It tells us if one has self-control or if they are disciplined. The list can go on.

Maybe we need to ask ourselves a question right now. Am I handling money right, or is money handling me? Sometimes bad times come, and we can't help it. It is out of our control, but then sometimes it is the way we have handled our finances. Too many credit cards, too many things we don't need, etc.

Money can cause a person to lose their right thinking and their common sense. Good people have turned ugly (bad) when money is in the picture or when they are in charge of money.

Oh yes, let us remember that, "The borrower is a servant to the lender." (Proverbs 22:7) The old cowboy said, "Once we are in debt to someone, we are carrying another man's weight. It will be him that sits in the saddle with his hands on the reigns." In other words, the lender will be in control.

Remember, money has a way of bringing out the best or the worst in us. Our tithing and giving to our local church is an expression of our gratitude (thankfulness) to God.

I like what Elder I. H. Terry taught me:

> Give God His tithe and offering.
> Save some.
> Eat some (buy food).
> Give some away.
> If you eat it all up, you are a glutton. If you give it all away, you are a fool. If you keep it all, you are an old miser.

Don't forget, one of these days we will come to the end of the road called Life. We need to make preparation for old age. Again, this is just a seed thought. I think you get the spirit of what we are talking about. I recommend Dave Ramsey's material on money and finances.

Lesson 45
The Time to Be Happy Is Now

There is a little song that says:

The time to be happy is now!
The place to be happy is here!
And the way to be happy is to make others happy
And to have a little heaven down here!

On this journey of life we need to work on being happy and doing our best to make others happy. Jesus said, "In the world ye shall have tribulation." (John 16:33) The word tribulation means trouble, pressure, burdened, suffer, affliction, tightness, distress, adversity and a trying experience. But Jesus went on to say, "but be of good cheer." (John 16:33) The word cheer means happy, hilarious, to be full of good spirits, a happy facial expression, to be merry, to dispel gloom and worry.

When Bro. Paul was before King Agrippa in Acts 26:2 he

said, "I think myself happy." We become what we think. "For as he thinketh in his heart, so is he." (Proverb 23:7)

We like to be happy. We want to be happy, and God wants us to be happy. Sometimes we have got to think ourselves happy. "I think" means that we have the rule over our thinking. We are the governor, and it means we can command our thinking.

So let's think Happy! Remember the time to be happy is now! Happy means to be joyous, enthusiastic, be blessed, contentment.

Blessed is every one that feareth the LORD; that walketh in his ways. For thou shalt eat the labour of thine hands: happy shalt thou be, and it shall be well with thee. (Psalms 128:1-2)

Happy is that people, that is in such a case: yea, happy is that people, whose God is the LORD. (Psalms 144:15)

Where there is no vision, the people perish: but he that keepeth the law, happy is he. (Proverbs 29:18)

He that handleth a matter wisely shall find good: and whoso trusteth in the LORD, happy is he. (Proverbs 16:20)

Happy is the man that findeth wisdom, and the man that getteth understanding. ... She is a tree of life to them that lay hold upon her: and happy is every one that retaineth her. (Proverbs 3:13, 18)

If ye know these things, happy are ye if ye do them. (Footwashing)(John 13:17)

The song says:
  We're a happy people. Yes, we are!
  We're a happy people. Yes, we are!
  Been baptized in Jesus Name.
  Spoke in tongues when the Holy Ghost came!
  We're a happy people. Yes, we are!

There are some Jesus Name Apostolics that need to go to McDonald's and get a happy meal! When the queen of Sheba went to see Solomon, she said, "The half was not told me." (I Kings 10:7) It says when she saw the house of the Lord, there was no more spirit in her. Then she said, "Happy are thy men, happy are these thy servants, blessed be the Lord thy God." (I Kings 10:8) When the unsaved come to our churches, they ought to see a happy people.

Leah, Jacob's wife said, "Happy am I." (Genesis 30:13) Can we say that? Are we a happy camper?

A merry heart doeth good like a medicine: but a broken spirit drieth the bones. (Proverbs 17:22)

A merry heart means a glad heart, a joyful heart a cheerful heart.

A merry heart maketh a cheerful countenance: (Proverbs 15:13)

All the days of the afflicted are evil: but he that is of a merry heart hath a continual feast. (Proverbs 15:15)

So, the time to be happy is now!

It is alright to laugh; to be happy and cheerful. The Bible says, "A time to weep, and a time to laugh." (Ecclesiastes 3:4) Sarah said, "God hath made me to laugh." (Genesis 21:6) The word "laugh" means to make merry, to rejoice, to laugh outright, or a sign of joy. The dictionary says that the word "laugh" means "to show joy with a smile or an explosive sound or to be of a kind that inspires joy." "God loveth a cheerful giver." (II Corinthians 9:7) Have you paid your tithes and offerings lately? If so, did you do it with a cheerful spirit? ☺ While Paul was facing death, even the Lord told Paul, "Be of good cheer." (Acts 23:11) In closing, remember the words of the song:

> The time to be happy is now!
> The place to be happy is here!
> And the way to be happy is to make others happy
> And to have a little heaven down here!

P.S. Go get a McDonald's Happy Meal if nothing else works. Oh yes, I just thought of something else..... I pastored a good man one time in his old age. His name was Bro. Anderson, and he was a character. He was an old time Apostolic. I came to church one night, and as I was going to the platform, he reached up and grabbed me by the arm and pulled me down. At that time he was in his 90's. He said, "Bro. Morton, I found a great big orange today, and I was going to bring it to you." I said, "Well, what did you do with it?" He said, "I ate it." I said to him, "Well it's a wonder you didn't bring me a big O'l lemon." He said, "Son, a lemon would sweeten you up." So if you don't like the McDonald's Happy Meal, go get yourself a lemon – it will probably sweeten you up! Be happy!

Lesson 46
Fulfilling Our Purpose

Here is another little thought that I have picked up on the road of life that has been a blessing. Think about this.

We are not here by chance, but by God's choosing. His hand formed us and made us the persons we are. God compares us to no one else. Remember the scripture, "They measuring themselves by themselves, and comparing themselves among themselves, are not wise." (2 Corinthians 10:12) So it is not wise for us to be in competition with others.

We are one of a kind according to God's design. We lack nothing that His grace can't give us. God has allowed us to be here at this time in history and in the kingdom of God, to fulfill His special purpose. Remember what the

Lord said unto the Apostle Paul, "I have appeared unto thee for this purpose." (Acts 26:16) Then the apostle wrote, "And we know that all things work together for good to them that love God, to them that are the called according to his purpose." (Romans 8:28)

To sum it all up, let me say, let's find the will of God for our life and do it with all of our heart. By doing the will of God we have found the purpose for our life.

Lesson 47
There's No Perfect Situation Life Is Full of Adjustments

Not that I speak in respect of want: for I have learned, in whatsoever state I am, therewith to be content. I know both how to be abased, and I know how to abound: every where and in all things I am instructed both to be full and to be hungry, both to abound and to suffer need. I can do all things through Christ which strengtheneth me. (Philippians 4:11–13)

In verse 11 the apostle said, "I have learned, in whatsoever state I am, therewith to be content." "Content" means to be happy or at ease. In other words, Bro. Paul was saying I have learned how to get along happily; to be at ease. I have learned how to be content with the condition I am in. We who know anything about the Apostle Paul know that he was in many adverse circumstances that were not pleasant. But he said, "I have learned to be content." An unhappy person is a miserable person. They are not happy with themselves and they can make those around them unhappy.

He said, "I have learned." "Learned" means to gain knowledge or understanding by experience. One thing that is very important, in fact, very, very important for us to learn is <u>there is no perfect situation</u>.

One man said, "I've yet to meet an absolute perfectionist whose life was filled with inner peace." Don't worry about being perfect. If we worry about being perfect, then we are not perfect. Cut yourself some slack.

We certainly want to do the best we can. Some people pride themselves on being a perfectionist. They can drive themselves crazy and make those around them very uncomfortable. I started working on this many years ago, when I got the revelation that there is no perfect situation, and I just needed to do the best I could.

Some people are always changing jobs because they are looking for the perfect job. There is no perfect job. There is no perfect school. There is no perfect husband. There is no perfect wife. There are no perfect children, and the list goes on and on. You get the idea.

If we are going to live in this life, we have to learn to get along with imperfection. I pastored in Fresno, California, for 41 and one half years and never did get it as perfect as I wanted it; but I didn't drive myself and the saints crazy trying to make everybody come to perfect perfection.

I know the Bible says, "Be ye therefore perfect, even as your Father which is in heaven is perfect." (Matthew 5:48) We may be perfect in God's eyes, but we will never be perfect in one another's eyes. So let's cut each other some slack.

"He that observeth the wind shall not sow; and he that regardeth the clouds shall not reap." (Ecclesiastes 11:4) In other words, the farmer that was looking for the perfect situation will never get anything done. God help us to learn that happiness is within us and not in our circumstances, and that there is no perfect situation. Relax.

I Never Got What I Wanted

It was spring,
But it was summer I wanted,
The warm days,
And the great outdoors.
It was summer,
But it was fall I wanted,
The colorful leaves,
And the cool, dry air.
It was fall,
But it was winter I wanted,
The beautiful snow,
And the joy of the holiday season.
It was winter,
But it was spring I wanted,
The warmth,
And the blossoming of nature.
I was a child,
But it was adulthood I wanted,
The freedom,
And the respect.
I was 20,
But it was 30 I wanted
To be mature,

I was middle-aged,
But it was 20 I wanted,
The youth,
And the free spirit.
I was retired,
But it was middle age I wanted,
The presence of mind,
Without limitations.
My life was over.
But I never got what I wanted.

Another little lesson I have learned is that:

Life is full of adjustments.

There is no way around it, about the time we get adjusted to one thing we have to adjust to another. Sometimes in life things happen to us that we do not like. It does not seem good, but life goes on. It is not always the same, so we have to learn to adjust. Remember, life is not going to adjust to us. We have to adjust to it.

Life starts out with adjustments. We adjust from the bottle to the cup to the glass. We adjust from crawling to walking. That is just the beginning, and you will have to use your own imagination and think of the many things we have had to adjust to in life.

One very important thing is we need to learn to adjust to the will of God, for the will of God is not going to adjust to us. Remember, life is full of adjustments. It is never over and there is no perfect situation. So relax!

Lesson 48
Timing

To every thing there is a season, and a time to every purpose under the heaven: (Ecclesiastes 3:1)

I returned, and saw under the sun, that the race is not to the swift, nor the battle to the strong, neither yet bread to the wise, nor yet riches to men of understanding, nor yet favour to men of skill; but time and chance happeneth to them all. (Ecclesiastes 9:11)

Our lesson today is on timing. The word timing according to the dictionary is:
- the time when something happens or is done; especially when it is thought of as having a good or bad effect on the result
- the ability to choose the best moment for some action or movement

- the ability to select the precise moment for doing something for the best effect

Timing is very important in life. Someone said timing is everything, so I want to talk about timing. You will have to sort it out. Timing is so important. God is a God of timing.

He hath made every thing beautiful in his time. (Ecclesiastes 3:11)

For there is a time there for every purpose and for every work. (Ecclesiastes 3:17)

A wise man's heart discerneth both time and judgment. Because to every purpose there is time and judgment. (Ecclesiastes 8:5-6)

There is truth in the old saying, "I was at the right place at the right time," or "I was at the wrong place at the wrong time." We can do the right thing at the wrong time and get in trouble. Sometimes we say, "I was just in time" or we may say "my timing was off." We can say, "If I had just been a minute sooner or later."

Waiting time can be a testing time. In life, at times, I have waited and waited and waited. Then all at once, it was time, and it happened. God seems to never get in a hurry. In fact, there is a lot in the Bible that talks about waiting on God. He never gets in a hurry, but He is never late. He always seems to be on time. Like the song says, "He's an on time God, yes, He is!"

Some people seem to have a gift for good timing. We say, "I was going to do it, but it just seems the timing was never right." Timing is everything. Timing is so important concerning jobs, houses, marriage, retirement, etc.

We must know God's time. "...because thou knewest not the time of thy visitation." (Luke 19:44)

To every thing there is a season, and a time to every purpose under the heaven: (Ecclesiastes 3:1)
...and a wise man's heart discerneth both time and judgment. (Ecclesiastes 8:5)

Remember, do the right thing at the right time, and God will bless. God's Will, God's Way, God's Time.

Lesson 49
Are We in Transition?

Transition:
Movement, passage, or change from one position, state, stage, subject, concept, etc., to another; change: or one place to another.

You may be reading this book and you are in transition, passing from one level of human experience to another. Life is filled with different situations that move us from one level to another. Willing or unwilling transition does take place. Sometimes life will call upon us to do something we have never done before. We must sometimes let go of the well-known. It can be hard to do.

When we move to another level, we may never go back to the same level as we were before. We may be moving into a new phase of life. It was said of Abraham, "By faith he sojourned in the land of promise, as in a strange country." (Hebrews 11:9) Anytime that we move into a new experience, it can be called a strange country for us.

It can be a minister that is a pastor and God is dealing with him. His time is up here. It is time to move on. It could be an evangelist whose time has come to settle down and be a pastor. It can be a young couple at the altar of marriage – making the transition from a single life to a married life – woe be unto you! Maybe you are just getting out of high school or college and you are making a transition. Maybe it is a new job, retirement, or something happening to us that we do not understand.

In transition, many times, there can be what we call the in-between time. In-between time can be a testing time. The Bible says to wait on the Lord.

In transition, we can be like Abraham. We need the assurance that God is with us. In transition, we can say, "Am I doing the right thing?" God said to Abraham, "After these things the word of the LORD came unto Abram in a vision, saying, Fear not, Abram: I am thy shield, *and* thy exceeding great reward." (Genesis 15:1) God was saying to Abraham that he was not alone in the transition, but that God was with him.

In transition we can have surprises. Nothing surprises God. Remember, you are called according to His purpose. There are no accidents with God. He is the one that put transition into motion.

In transition, in the in-between times, we must ask God, "What do you want to say to me in this? What is the lesson that I must learn? What am I to do from this point on?"

For my thoughts are not your thoughts, neither are your ways my ways, saith the LORD. (Isaiah 55:8)

"Jesus answered and said unto him, What I do thou knowest not now; but thou shalt know hereafter." (John 13:7) Sometimes in transition, we do not know what God is doing, but at the right time it will all come together. It is important to be <u>very patient</u> in times of transition.

Lesson 50
Winning

It takes a little courage
And a little self-control,
And some grim determination
If you want to reach your goal
It takes a deal of striving,
And a firm and stern-set chin,
No matter what the battle,
If you're really out to win.

There's no easy path to glory,
There's no rosy road to fame,
Life, however we may view it,
Is no simple parlor game;
But its prizes call for fighting,
For endurance and for grit,
For a rugged disposition
And a "don't-know-when-to-quit"

You must take a blow or give one,
You must risk and you must lose,
And expect that in the struggle
You will suffer from a bruise.
But you mustn't wince or falter,
If a fight you once begin,
Be a man and face the battle –
That's the only way to win.
~ Author Unknown

Lesson 51
Working Through the Process

He that doeth the will of God abideth forever.
(I John 2:17)

How do we find the will of God? How do we know what is right? What is the will of God? If it is in the Bible, then we know. We know what to do and what the will of God is.

How do we come to what is right? "And in process of time it came to pass." (Genesis 4:3) "In process of time." (Genesis 38:12) "And it came to pass in process of time." (Exodus 2:23) "And it came to pass in process of time." (Judges 11:4) The key word here is PROCESS. So our subject is working through the process. Say it with me - "Working Through The Process!"

This is a revelation that can help us in knowing what to do. As we make this journey of life, we are working through the process. The word "process" means working to an end, to subject to a special process, to move in a procession, to proceed, a continuous operation, a forward movement, to complete the whole course, a change that leads toward a particular result.

In other words, we work through the process until we come to the answer. The answer may be yes, no, or wait. Working through the process sometimes, in fact, takes time and patience. Jesus said "In your patience possess ye your souls." (Luke 21:19) "Wait on the LORD: be of good courage, and he shall strengthen thine heart: wait, I say, on the LORD." (Psalms 27:14) "My soul, wait thou only upon God; for my expectation is from him." (Psalms 62:5)

In the course of time, or shall we say "in the process of time," the answer will come. Working through the process can be about many things.

- Finding the will of God for our life
- Job
- The purchase of a house
- Car
- About our Children
- Moving
- A husband
- A Wife
- Etc.....

We do need to pray about everything, for the Bible says, "In all thy ways acknowledge him, and he shall direct thy paths." (Proverbs 3:6)

We have to give it time to go through the process. In other words, be patient. In pastoring for many years, I have helped many, many people work through many, many things. This is the way I do it, you may be comfortable doing it another way. I start with the word of God.

Trust in the LORD with all thine heart; and lean not unto thine own understanding. In all thy ways acknowledge him, and he shall direct thy paths. (Proverbs 3:5, 6)

In other words He, God, will help us work through the process until we come to His will. The reason I start with the Bible is because Jeremiah 10:23 says, "I know that the way of man is not in himself: it is not in man that walketh to direct his steps."

We need God to help us work through the process. The next thing I do is say, "God, this is my plan. I am going to start working through the process. Let me know if this is right or not." We cannot go into the process with a made up mind. We must remain open to the will of God. We must pray continually, "Thy will be done, O God." We must not give in to the pressures from people's opinions or our own ambitions. We must seek counsel from the right people in our life such as pastor, father, mother, husband, wife, etc.

We should seek counsel from people who have succeeded in the area we are working through. We must consider all of our options and be willing to use any one of them. We must have a plan, but be willing to change our plan. In other words, working through the process is like putting something in escrow. It has to go through the process.

In Genesis 24, the servant of Abraham, in seeking a wife for Isaac, prayed and worked through the process and he found a bride for his master's son. Even in the corporate world, companies, big and small, in buying and selling, and doing business, use the method of working through the process. The method of working through the process has helped me for many, many years to find the will of God or the right answer. I have found in life there are many decisions to be made and much to work through.

"Being confident of this very thing, that he which hath begun a good work in you will perform it until the day of Jesus Christ." (Philippians 1:6) This means that God wants to finish the course with us. God will not get tired and quit halfway through the process, nor will He renege on His promises. He will continue the process with us as long as we let Him, until He gets us to where He is taking us.

And he came out, and went, as he was wont, to the Mount of Olives; and his disciples also followed him. And when he was at the place, he said unto them, Pray that ye enter not into temptation. And he was withdrawn from them about a stone's cast, and kneeled down, and prayed, Saying, Father, if thou be willing, remove this cup from me: nevertheless not my will, but thine, be done. And there appeared an angel unto him from heaven, strengthening him. And being in an agony he prayed more earnestly: and his sweat was as it were great drops of blood falling down to the ground. (Luke 22:39-44)

What is Jesus doing here? He is working through the process.

The story is told of a man on an African safari deep in the jungle. The guide before him had a machete and was whacking away the tall weeds and thick underbrush. The traveler, wearied and hot, asked in frustration, "Where are we? Do you know where you are taking me? Where is the path?!" The seasoned guide stopped and looked back at the man and replied, "I am the path."

We ask the same questions, don't we? We ask God, "Where are you taking me? Where is the path on this journey?" He answers, "I am the Way. I am the path. Just follow me." We can find the way if we will be patient and prayerful and be willing to work through the process.

AN OPEN DOOR

As we make our way through life, we must be careful not to open doors that God does not want us to go through. As we are walking down the street and we come to a door, and it is opened, that does not mean that we are supposed to enter in. I like what Bro. Paul said, "I came to Troas to preach Christ's gospel, and a door was opened unto me of the Lord." (II Corinthians 2:12) It is much better when God opens the door. We must not force the door, we must let God lead. It really is something, isn't it, feeling our way through life, working through the process? I hope this little lesson helps you stay in the will of God or find the will of God. It is up to you now.

Lesson 52
The Present Duty Is the Will of God

Concerning the will of God for our life, some people are always looking way out there. They are looking for it and never finding it. An old friend of mine, Pastor Bill Barnes, taught me a lesson many years ago. He said simply this, "The present duty is the will of God." This little thought is so simple that we will miss it if we are not careful. To explain this let me say, we just get up every day and whatever needs to be done, we do it. We pray, we have our devotion, we make a list of things to be done for that day, and it can be many things. By doing that every day, we will be in the will of God. God can direct our path. The problem is some people think the will of God is some great big thing they will find in the future. But really, the everyday duty is God's Will.

- If you see a piece of paper, pick it up.
- If you see something that needs to get done, do it.
- If the car needs to be washed, wash it.
- If the shoes need to be shined, shine them.
- If the church needs to be cleaned, clean it.

I think you get the point. Whatever needs to be done right now, do it. It is the present duty, and this is the Will of God. So journey on, and this will bring you to where you belong in life.

Lesson 53
The Will of God Is Not Always Comfortable

Some people think that the will of God is always a comfortable place filled with tranquility, but that is not always so. For example, remember Jesus prayed in the garden, and He said, "Father, if it be possible, let this cup pass from me: nevertheless not as I will, but as thou wilt." (Matthew 26:39) Calvary was the will of God, but it was not comfortable. The Bible says in Isaiah 53 that, He was despised, rejected of men, a man of sorrows, and acquainted with grief. He carried our griefs and our sorrows. He was wounded for our transgressions, and He poured out his soul unto death. They put a crown of thorns about His head. They mocked Him, spit upon Him, and smote Him. They came to a place called Golgotha - a place of a skull. They gave Him vinegar to drink and then crucified Him. This doesn't sound very comfortable to me, but it was the will of God. As you are reading this page you may be very uncomfortable, yet in the will of God. Think about what the men of God in the Old Testament and the Apostles in the New Testament suffered and went through, yet it was the will of God. They could have been saying, "This is not comfortable. I do not like this. I am leaving. I am moving. I am getting out of this." They had to find the inner peace in the midst of tribulation and come to the conclusion that this is the will of God for me.

The main thing is to have that inner peace no matter what we are going through. Though it is uncomfortable, this is God's will for me.

P.S. Sometimes we as preachers think that if circumstances are not comfortable, we are not in the Will of God. This is not always so. I have been in uncomfortable circumstances, but I had inner peace. Though it is not comfortable, it is God's Will for me right now. Like the Apostle Paul said, "I have learned, in whatever state I am, therewith to be content."

Lesson 54
You Will Know It When You See It

Another little lesson that I have learned on the road of life, is a story that has blessed me. I don't remember if I read it somewhere, or heard it somewhere or where I got it. I just remember it came to me.

The story goes like this…

There was a man who was an artist. He painted pictures of beautiful scenes for a living. He would paint and sell his paintings. He loved beautiful scenery and would paint it. Sadly, way down in his heart he was never satisfied. He was always looking for that special scenery that he could paint and be totally satisfied.

So one day he decided to go for a ride. As he was riding through the hills, he saw a dirt road that he had never been on before. So he turned and traveled up the road with its twists and turns and finally he came to the end of the road.

There at the end of the road was a place to turn around. As he turned around he saw an apple orchard. Up through the apple orchard he saw a house. He looked and there at the edge of the road and the orchard was a little spring of water, a table and four chairs. On the table was a pitcher, four glasses and a bowl of apples. This all caught his eye. All at once there appeared an elderly man, dressed in his work clothes. He stopped and said, "Howdy!"

The artist was curious about the table, chairs, the pitcher and the fruit. So the artist stopped and turned off his car.

The farmer said, "Get out and rest yourself."

So as curious as the artist was he got out, and he asked him concerning the table, the chairs and the fruit.

The old farmer said, "Well it's like this, ever so often we have people just like you come up this old dirt road, and as you can see this is the end of the road. Several years back I decided to put this table, chairs, pitcher and fruit out here. If you will notice there's a spring of water here. I wanted people to stop and get a cool drink and eat a delicious apple. Some mighty good folks have passed this way, and I have met some fine people."

The artist asked him, "Have you lived here long?"

He said, "My grandfather owned this place, then my dad, and now me and my wife. My grandpa and folks have long passed away. We grow these apples and love this place." Then the farmer said, "By the way, Son, what do you do for a living?"

The artist replied, "I am an artist. I paint scenery. I sell my paintings for a living. I love it." The artist and the farmer talked for a bit. Then the farmer said, "Right up the foot path there is a real beautiful scene." Then he said, "I must be getting back to the house, I've got things to do."

The artist asked, "Do you mind if I walk up the path and see the beautiful scene that you were talking about?"

The farmer said, "No, make yourself at home and stay as long as you wish."

The artist turned and started up the path and in a few feet he turned back to the elderly farmer and said, "That scene that you were talking about, where is it?"

The old farmer said, "<u>Son, you will know it when you see it</u>." The old farmer turned and walked away. The artist walked up the path and through the woods, and all at once he rounded a big rock and there it was. The most beautiful scene that he had ever looked upon.

Immediately he said in his heart, "This is what I have been looking for!" There was a peace and tranquility that came to the artist. "I must paint this scene."

And so it is in life, we pray, we think, we search, we meditate, we counsel. It can be one of many things that we are trying to find the will of God about. All at once, we may have been looking for it a long time or a short time or whatever. There it is, but we know THIS IS THE WILL OF GOD. We must make sure that it is God's will and not ours. All I know is, that in my life, I get that certain feeling when it is right.

There was a time in my life that I had evangelized for four years, but for the last couple of years I was searching for the will of God - when and where to settle down. I won't go through all the circumstances, but all at once one day, it unfolded and... "I knew it when I saw it." <u>I pray if you are searching for the will of God today, that when you see it, you will know it</u>.

The Bridge Builder
By Will Allen Dromgoole

An old man going a lone highway,
Came, at the evening cold and gray,
To a chasm vast and deep and wide.
Through which was flowing a sullen tide
The old man crossed in the twilight dim,
The sullen stream had no fear for him;
But he turned when safe on the other side
And built a bridge to span the tide.

"Old man," said a fellow pilgrim near,
"You are wasting your strength with building here;
Your journey will end with the ending day,
You never again will pass this way;
You've crossed the chasm, deep and wide,
Why build this bridge at evening tide?"

The builder lifted his old gray head;
"Good friend, in the path I have come," he said,
"There followed after me to-day
A youth whose feet must pass this way.
This chasm that has been as naught to me
To that fair-haired youth may a pitfall be;
He, too, must cross in the twilight dim;
Good friend, I am building this bridge for him!"

And thine ears shall hear a word behind thee, saying, this is the way, walk ye in it, (Isaiah 30:21)

Lesson 55
A Good Understanding Makes for Long Time Friends

On this road called Life we want some longtime friends; which is a very very good thing. For this to happen we must have a good understanding. That means we have got to learn to communicate.

Communication means an act of transmitting, or to transmit one's thoughts to another. Bro. Paul said, "Seeing then that we have such hope, <u>we use great plainness of speech</u>." (II Corinthians 3:12)

Sometimes I have walked away from a person thinking, "What did they mean? Did I understand them right?" I like what it says in Luke 24. Here we have two of the disciples on what we call the Emmaus road. Verse 15 says, "they communed together and reasoned," and in verse 17

Jesus said to them, "What manner of communications are these that ye have one to another, as ye walk?"

Some people are better communicators than others. Some speak very plain. There is no doubt as to what they are saying. In other words, they tell it like it is and you understand it. Others, as the old saying goes, "beat around the bush." Others don't like to speak up because they have a spirit of fear. Bro. Paul said, "For God hath not given us the spirit of fear." (2 Timothy 1:7)

How many problems could have been worked out if two people would have just communicated? The old cowboy said, "It is better to talk it out than to shoot it out." I say again, we must learn to communicate, so there will be a good understanding.

Sometimes we think the other person is thinking the same as we are, but they are not. That can cause trouble. We think one way and they think another way. The words can be the same but they mean different things. <u>We need good communication or plainness of speech</u>.

I am not teaching against texting, so don't get me wrong. However, too many people today, instead of going to the person face to face, they send a text. What they really need to do is sit down with the person face to face. Feel their spirit, see their expressions and communicate. Talk it out not text it out. <u>We preachers, especially pastors, must not deal with spiritual things by texting. Technology is not to take the place of the personal touch</u>.

Right now you may know of a situation that could be worked out with communication and a good understanding. Again I say, on this road called Life, to have and keep longtime friends, we must learn to communicate.

The Lord said, "Come now, and let us reason together." (Isaiah 1:18) That is communication.

P.S. I trust I have communicated this lesson correctly!

Lesson 56
Old Friends

The scripture says, "Thine own friend, and thy father's friend forsake not." (Proverbs 27:10) There is nothing like friends. There is especially nothing like old friends, which have stuck with you through thick and thin. It brings to my mind a song that Sis. Cathy Clark sat down at the piano and began to play and sing. This was a long time ago, when we were gathered together with some old friends.

Old Friends

Old friends, after all of these years
Just old friends, through the laughter and tears
Old friends, what a find, what a priceless treasure
Old friends, like a rare piece of gold
My old friends, brought me in from the cold
Old friends, through it all I will hold to old friends.

God must have known that some days on our own
We would lose the will to go on
That's why he sent friends like you along

Old friends, yes, you've always been there
My old friends, we've had more than our share
Old friends, I'm a rich millionaire in old friends

A cold snowy sleigh ride, or carols at midnight
A box someone left at my door
A bell ringing just to remind me to care for the poor
Some shepherds and angels, a babe in a manger
A secret that had to be told
How God made us friends is a story that never grows old.
~ By Bill Gaither

It is very important on this journey called Life that we have and keep some old friends.

"If I had a flower for every time I thought of you,
I could walk through my garden forever."

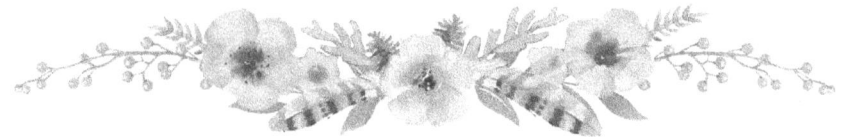

I would have loved to meet the person who inspired this quote. Nothing feels better than to be loved, except maybe to be in love. Life and love are so precious. Don't ever take either for granted.

People walk into our lives every day. The hard truth is that some of those people will walk right back out. We'll think of them, we'll miss them, we'll wonder what might have been, but sometimes we just have to let them go.

A special few will leave wrinkles that run deep into the fabric of our hearts. The kind of wrinkles that can never really be ironed out. For better or for worse, they will always be a part of who we are. It can hurt when they're gone, but rather than be sad, we need to be thankful that we were blessed with their companionship even if just for a blink of an eye.

And as for those who are in our lives today? Let's not wait another minute to let them know how much we love and appreciate them.

Have faith. Love deeply. Always, always, always forgive.

~David G. Weber
Chief Operating Officer
The Association of Mature American Citizens

Long and Winding Road
By Mickey Mangun

When I made my start for heaven.
I could only find one way.
A road that lead me through the mountains and valleys,
A road not many folks could take.
Since I started traveling on my journey,
I've covered many, many miles behind me.
Miles of sun and rain.
Miles of smiles and pain.
This road's been rough,
but I again would choose the same.

Long and Winding Road
Keep on leading me
Up ahead I see a sign that tells me
you're heading straight for your victory.
I know I must be traveling right
for I remember passing Calvary
Although it's dusty and it's old,
For years it's born the traveler's load.
Someday this road will turn to gold.

There are sometimes when the rocks hurt my feet,
My body burns from the sweat and the heat,
My strength completely drains,
Until my face marks the pain,
My back gets bent from the strain,
Oh! Now I could turn around
For the road is still there,
But every mountain that I've climbed,
I again would have to bear.

And so I really can't turn back.
Some may be using my tracks
I see one more bend
and that just might be my road's end.

Long and Winding Road
Keep on leading me
Up ahead I see a sign that tells me
You're heading straight for your victory.
I know I must be traveling right
For I remember passing Calvary.
Although it's dusty and it's old,
For years it's born the traveler's load.
Someday this road will turn to gold.

May The Road Rise Up To Meet You

May the road rise up to meet you.
May the wind be always at your back.
May the sun shine warm upon your face;
The rains fall soft upon your fields
And until we meet again,
May God hold you in the palm of His hand.
~ Irish Blessing

On your journey, may God be with you wherever life takes you on this "Road Called Life." I have written this book because I care. Happy Trails to you until we meet again.

Very Sincerely,

Elder Vaughn Morton

About the Author

Elder Vaughn Morton was not born or raised in Pentecost. In 1955, he repented of his sins, was baptized in Jesus name and filled with the Holy Ghost at the age of 15. He wholeheartedly embraced the Apostolic Pentecostal life as taught by his pastor, J.E. Rode. He worked faithfully with Bro. Rode in Modesto, California for four years until God opened the door to enter full time ministry in 1960. From that time until now, he has raised two sons, pastored a total of 44 and one-half years and evangelized 12 years. He has four grandsons and two granddaughters.

His journey not only in ministry, but the consistent living for God day after day, year after year, has brought about these practical lessons. Those closest to Elder Morton through the years have enjoyed and cherished his practical teaching. In this book you will find simple, yet inspiring, phrases and lessons to apply to your journey that will help you on *The Road Called Life*.

www.ingramcontent.com/pod-product-compliance
Lightning Source LLC
Chambersburg PA
CBHW040415100526
44588CB00022B/2837